Chronicles

of a

Betrothed

Chronicles

of a

Betrothed

By
Annetta Hobson

dpInk
Donnalnk Publications, L.L.C.

Donnalnk Publications, L.L.C.
Through former sole proprietorship, "The Book Nook / Donnalnk Publications."
4405 S. Kirkman Rd. Suite #B208, Orlando, FL 32811
Visit our website at www.donnaink.org

This book is a work of fiction. Names, characters, places, and incidents are the product of the author's imagination or are used fictitiously. Any resemblance to actual events, locales, or persons, living or dead, is coincidental.

Copyright © 2014 by Donnalnk Publications, L.L.C. for Annetta Hobson.
Cover art © 2014 by Donnalnk Publications, L.L.C. for Annetta Hobson created by Sarah Foster, Sprinkles on Top Studios, United States of America.

All rights reserved. In accordance with the *U.S. Copyright Act of 1976*, the scanning, uploading and electronic sharing of any part of this book without the permission of the publisher is unlawful piracy and theft of the author's intellectual property. If you would like to use material from the book (other than for review purposes), prior written permission must be obtained by contacting the publisher at permissions@donnaink.org.

Donnalnk Publications, L.L.C. and logo are trademarks of Donna Ink, a flagship company. The publisher is not responsible for websites (or their content) not owned by the publisher.

Cover Design: Donnalnk Publications, L.L.C. Sarah Foster, Sprinkles on Top Studios. Editorial Team: Donnalnk Publications, L.L.C., Mr. Quante Bryan; ZenCon an Art of Zen Consultancy, Ms. Dana Queen. Layout and Design: Ms. Dana Queen.

First Paperback Edition: August 2014. First Electronic Edition: August 2014.

Library of Congress Cataloging in Publication Data:

Annetta Hobson, 2014 -
    Chronicles of a Betrothed / Hobson, Annetta. - 1st ed.
                                       ISBN: 978-1-939425-43-0 (print aka)
    262 p.cm.

Summary: "19 year old Chakori Desai is the daughter of Prime Minister Roshan Desai. To end a devastating and annihilating battle between their war stricken islands, he offers Chakori to Monarch Pavan Khattris to marry his son, Daler Khattris. Before she can protest, Chakori is faced with a dilemma. Should she give in to desire or retain her moral sense of right and wrong?" ~ Summary provided by the author.

[1. Literature - Fiction, 2. Romance - Fiction, 3. Adult Relationships - Fiction, 4. Erotica – Fiction, 5. Thriller – Fiction, 6. Dramatic – Fiction, 7. United States – Fiction, 8. Women's Literature - Fiction.]

I. Title. II. Title: Reverse Seduction
Dewey Classification: 813
10 9 8 7 6 5 4 3 2 1

2014949732

Printed in the United States of America.

Contents

Contents i
Other Titles by iii
Annetta Hobson iii
Acknowledgement v
Dedication vii
Chapter 1 1
Chapter 2 11
Chapter 3 21
Chapter 4 33
Chapter 5 45
Chapter 6 55
Chapter 7 67
Chapter 5 73
Chapter 8 87
Chapter 9 97
Chapter 10 107
Chapter 11 117
Chapter 12 127
Chapter 13 139
Chapter 14 157

Annetta Hobson

Chapter 15	169
Chapter 16	181
Chapter 17	191
Chapter 18	203
Chapter 19	213
Chapter 20	223
Chapter 21	237
About the Author	243
Visit the Author	245
Social Media	245
Blog and Websites	245
Publisher	245

Other Titles by
Annetta Hobson

Chronicles of a Betrothed
Light in the Shadow
Light in the Shadow, Part II
Pretty Dreamer
Reverse Seduction
The Flame
Weather Vain

Acknowledgement

I would like to acknowledge my niece Aneisha Norman for being as excited about this story as I am, my husband for giving me the governmental elements of the plot. My best friend Vivian McClendon for always encouraging me, and my wonderful sister Anetris Norman-Williams for being there in the middle of the night to help. Last but not least, I would like to thank DonnaInk Publications, L.L.C. for taking a chance on me and aiding in reaching the world of readers. You are responsible for making my dream come true.

Dedication

I would like to dedicate this novel to all of my readers. I hope that I can always write things you want to read.

Chronicles of a Betrothed

Chapter 1

The war between our islands date as far back as I can remember. I am 19 years of age and the war continues to wage on. The Island of Jutesh and Ghatlan have been enemies for the length of my years. I believe the battle has been fought even longer.

My father inherited a heap of troubles from the former Prime minister. The war had no end in sight and no way for us to win. We were outnumbered and overpowered. The order of business for my father was to call for help. The United Countries sent several thousand soldiers to man our Island of 50,000. I prayed every night for my father to arrive home safe and secure. The morning of the fifth day in June, I awake from a restless slumber. I tossed and turned until the light crept through the crack in my silk woven gold colored curtains. The glare hurt my eyes. I had been staring at the ceiling, at least what I could make out, all evening. Slowly the sunlight peeks in and spreads throughout the room, lightly brushing my lids. I shield my face and hurry to remedy the problem. As I turn to stumble back to my bed Yashica enters my room. "Chakori your father requests your presence immediately."

"And, what is it exactly that he needs?"

"I guess you will have to get dressed and go find out."

Annetta Hobson

Yashica is our beloved maid and caregiver for as many years as my mind could travel. My mother trusted her with I and my little brother's lives. And, because of the war she had several escapes planned for our urgent departure if necessary. I bath and dress to prepare for the unexpected conference with the Prime Minister of Ghatlan. I walk with complete ease down the long and narrowed hall. I can hear the voices of several people descending from the office. I take a quick peek in the intimidating room before I enter.

"Oh yes, here she is. My beautiful daughter Chakori Desai of Ghatlan." My father states as he smiles nervously and stands to greet me.

I kiss his cheek and lean in to embrace him and I can feel his heart beating so fast it threatens to burst from his chest. I nod to the five gentleman in the room and turn back to my father. "What is this father? I am never allowed in your political meetings." There is that nervous smile again.

"Chakori sit please."

I smile back at him and slowly take a seat. I survey the room. There are men of importance present. I just don't understand why I am.

A tall dark man with ear length wavy hair stands and clears his throat. "I am Pavan Khattris, the Monarch of Jutesh. I and your family have come to a truce. I want to extend my apology for the turmoil we have caused your land."

My mouth opens and I cover it with my hand.

"Thank you Sir." I say removing it before turning ignorantly towards my father. "Father..."

"Wait Kori. You have to hear Monarch Khattris out."

Chronicles of a Betrothed

I turn back to the heartless tyrant who had riddled my Island with destruction since my birth.

He smiles a devilish and evil grin. He is quite handsome. But how can any woman desire such a man.

"Mistress Desai. I am here to collect you and your things. We are traveling back to Jutesh in the morning."

"Pardon me?" I say not comprehending what it is he is trying to convey.

"Let me cut in now Sir." My father interrupts. "Chakori." He says as he approaches. He grabs my arms and kisses my forehead.

"My beautiful sun flower, I love you with all my heart. But the people of Ghatlan are suffering and the soldiers for the United Countries need rest. I am signing a Treaty with Monarch Pavan. And the major seal of the treaty is your hand to his son, in one year from today."

Fear chokes me. Sadness overcomes me. I am at a loss of words. My father has just revealed to me that I was the barter in a treaty agreement. I do not speak. Anger is beginning to course through my veins. I turn away so that the tyrant does not get the satisfaction of witnessing my tears. "Father how could you? What does Mother say about this?"

"There is nothing to say. I am the leader of this land and I have done what's best."

"For whom? You want to save your own a . ."

"Chakori! You dare speak to your father in that tone!"

'Smack!' I soar across the room. The chair that was once beneath me lies on the floor. The evil Tyrant has begun his management of me. I grab my cheek and the waterworks flow. "Father." I sob. But he turns away to leave the room.

"I apologize, Monarch Khattris. She will be prepared to leave by morning. She is 19 years of age and intelligent. She will make a fine wife to your son and mother of your descendants. She has had the finest educators in all of our land. And, she is well trained in the duties that have to be performed as a wife. Our women are taught from the ripe age of 9 to cook clean and sew. Your son will have to train her in her other duties."

"Oh yes he will handle her fine. But she will not be given to him until after they have wed. This I promise." My father nods at him and firmly grips his hand. They shake and the entourage of suits leaves the mansion.

"Yashica! Come! Collect my daughter. Prepare her for her departure."

"Yes sir. Right away."

She grabs my arms and lifts me. She wraps her arm firmly around me and we start down the hall to bid my life goodbye.

I start to pack away my fine garments, one after the other. Tears roll down my cheek and plop onto my bags. I wipe the salty water from my lips. As I sort through the pile, I come across my gown that I wore to my coming of age ball. The first family always celebrates at the age of 16. It is given at the island's Grand Hall. The multitude of soldiers that stood outside to protect us that night was unbelievable. The door of my room opening breaks me from my daydream. I turn to see who has entered but the tears in my eyes have blurred my vision. I wipe them and I am bombarded with affection. I blink and it is the love of my life, Elliot.

Chronicles of a Betrothed

"Oh God, Kori. Please tell me this is a rumor."

"No Elliot, it is no rumor. The war is over and my Betrothal is the reason."

He gasps. A single tear forms in the corner of his eye. He grabs me closer. His hands linger in my hair as he inhales. I let my hair loose before I began packing, which is a major crime in my family. Our hair is to remain pinned in a secure roll at all times. Only when we sleep is it to be unbound. Elliot loves when I release it. It tumbles down my back and kisses my bottom. He is pure, straight from the United Countries. He was 18 when I met him. He had just enrolled for the duties. When he first approached me I knew it was wrong and that my father would never approve. But after months of him chasing me I gave in. My father allowed him to guard the family home unaware of our deception. Yashica knows but she would never betray my trust. I wanted to marry him one day. But I guess that is no longer an option. We are not allowed to have any sort of physical interactions until we are married and that is something I honor. I believe Elliot understands and would never try and counter it.

"Kori how will I live without you? I wake each day with anticipation. My heart beats just to get a glimpse of you. This cannot be happening."

I look to the floor. "I don't know. This arrangement will end a long waged war. I have to."

"That is not your responsibility! These are not your people, they are your father's responsibility!"

I lightly touch his lips. He closes his eyes.

"But they are my people. We are one in the same. My mother is here and my brother. What am I to do?"

Annetta Hobson

"I can't do this. I love you Chakori and I will never let you go!"

"Shhh. You cannot go against my father you will lose." He presses his forehead to mine and we stand there not speaking for a while. Then there is a tap on my door. I jump and he runs to hide.

"Chakori, I have something for you." My mother says as she enters.

"Mother, why? Can't you do something?"

"No my darling. This is the way we settled things in the old days. Your husband would have been chosen regardless. It is just now you have to move to his island."

"I cannot believe you would just hand me over to a man who has been trying to kill our family since father was elected."

"My dear child. There are certain aspects of politics you will never understand. Just don't try. Be a good wife. Bare as many children as you can. The Khattris family are a very, very wealthy family."

"I don't care about that, we are wealthy."

"But we have never been able to enjoy it. Now we all can live comfortably, without threats of being killed. Besides their wealth outweighs ours 7 to 1."

I am in shock. My mother is speaking as if I am going off to vacation. I can't believe they are unconcerned.

"Here you are my dear. Wear this." She places a sterling silver bracelet around my wrist. It has diamonds covering it. She clamps it and sighs. "It was your great grandmother's. When you look at it you will think of us. Give him lots of children, do whatever he asks and keep him happy. Maybe he will let you visit sometimes."

The callousness coming from my mother is ripping me apart inside. She has always been a gentle sweet woman. The person presented in front of me this day is a shadow of her.

"Why is your hair unbound? Turn around." She grabs a brush from my armoire and begins to brush my hair. She winds it around her hand and twists it into a tight bun. She holds it in place as she stands and grabs a long fancy pin to fasten it in place.

"There. You look perfect. We will see you off tomorrow. Don't do anything to ruin this. The people of this island can finally live in peace."

My hearts breaks into pieces as she speaks. I just wish she would go. I don't want to say anything else to upset her, so I just want her to leave my room.

"I will go now. But remember what I said. Plus I hear The Khattris' son is very handsome. You are in for a treat." She smiles and leaves the room.

Elliot emerges from hiding, gloom has taken his face.

I open my arms and he steps in. I hold him and he holds me. Tears build and soon I am sobbing uncontrollably. "What am I going to do? I don't want to marry that awful man's son. He is a murderer."

"Let's run! Run far away. We can go to the United Countries. What do you think?"

I ponder for a moment. "I don't know. If we get caught you will be killed."

"I will be nothing if you leave. So I mind as well die." I jump into his arms and he holds me into place.

"Let's go!" I grab some of my things.

"No leave everything! I have a little money we can buy new things."

I drop my bag and we run for my door. I stop and peek out of it. No one is around. Now that the treaty is signed there are no soldiers afoot. We run down the hall and hear voices as we turn the corner. I dip into the library and pull him behind me. We hide alongside a book case.

"I don't trust him Roshan. I know you are the leader of this land, but are you sure you are doing what is best for your daughter?"

"Marya. Please do not meddle in political affairs. I know what is best for everyone and that is more important than anything else."

"With our daughter in his domain, he has power over us my dear husband. He will use Chakori as a tool to control us. Watch and see."

"I will not ask you again to stay out of the affairs of my land."

They walk down the stairs and their voices can no longer be heard. I step from behind the case. Elliot looks at me and we dart back into the hall and down the back stairs. We creep to the service entrance and out of the door. I search for a possible vehicle to get away in and spot a utility truck. I race to the door and open it. I tilt the visor and a pair of keys drop onto the seat. Elliot shoves me in and pushes me over. I slide to the passenger side of the front seat and he starts the engine. He slams the door tight and we take off.

"Ok now what?" I ask instantly feeling regret as I watch the mansion where I grew into a woman disappears in the rear view mirror.

"Now we lay low until the freight ship arrives to carry the soldiers and their equipment home."

My stomach starts to turn. I know I must do this. But it feels like I am betraying my people. The Tyrant will kill my family.

"No Elliot, stop, turn around. Khattris will kill my Father. I know he will."

Chapter 2

"Chakori, you will never see anyone from this island again. The United Countries are far, far away. We had never heard of this place there until we came to fight. So sit back my love and ponder on the fact that soon we will be married and we will have many, many children."

I laugh. The thought of marrying Elliot and having his children delighted me. I could not think of anything better.

"Your family does not care about you. They only want to end the war."

"Actually, that is all I dream about Elliot, the war being over. I wanted to have a family here, with you."

"Well now, it's just a change of venue, that's all."

I smile as I watch Elliot drive the truck. I know my life with him will be bitter sweet. I will one day marry the love of my life. But I will lose my family and my heritage.

"Turn here." I point as Elliot turns the wheel. The truck tips as it bends the winding road.

"Where are we Chakori?"

I grab his hand and gently caress my face with it. He glides it along my jaw and turn to look at me.

Annetta Hobson

"I love you more than I have ever loved anyone in my life. You are my future and no one, I mean no one will take you from me. Not even a murderous Tyrant." The thought of Khattris sends spine tingling chills down my back. *If he finds us we will surely die.*

"Here we are." I say. We both look up at the decayed building the truck rests in front of. "I remember this place. It is where I first kissed you."

"Yes. Khattris had it destroyed a few years back. I still come here to be alone with my thoughts. My family will not think to look here."

"Alright. Now I have the food we will need." He jumps from the vehicle. He hurries to the back and open the hatch. There are several meal packets for the soldiers. "It should last us for about a week. The freight should be here by then."

I step out of the truck and rap my arms around myself. "I hope we are not discovered."

"We won't. You said it yourself. They will not look here.

We set up a small camp in the basement of the dilapidated building. The supplies from the truck must have been for a soldier station. Everything we needed to survive was available. Elliot prepares the area for us to sleep. He unfolds the tightly bound bundle. It is a ball of what appears to be some sort of sleeping bag. He takes several of them and aligns them along the wall. He fluffs and straightens the stack. It appears to be comfortable enough for us to sleep. I should have thought this out further. We have no food, water, nor anything else we would need to live for a week. Thank the Gods we stole a soldier utility vehicle or this getaway would have failed.

Chronicles of a Betrothed

"What are you thinking about my love?" Elliot calmly asks as he sits on the make shift bed.

"I am just very happy this soldier's utility vehicle was newly stocked."

Elliot head drops. He sighs and sadness washes over his face.

"What? What is it Elliot?"

"I am so sorry Chakori but I have deceived you."

"I don't understand."

"The truck is mine. It is fully stocked because I stocked it. My plan all along was to whisk you away to The United Countries."

My mouth drops open. I am surprised.

"How did you know I would come with you?"

"We love one another. There was never a doubt. You will be my wife, forever until death."

I smile. The thought of living a quiet uncomplicated life is all I desire. I will be a mother and a wife. Not the daughter of a diplomat anymore. I will be Mrs. Elliot Lockhart of the United Countries, a soldier's bride. Nothing more.

"Come my sweet. Lie here next to me. I want you in my arms."

I take a step toward him. I unravel my arms and drop them to my side. I straighten my tunic and smooth the ruffles from my skirt caused by the wild ride to our nest, our new sanctuary. The place where it all began.

I sit next to him. I am shaking like a leaf blowing in the evening breeze. My hands are so unsteady, he grabs me and pulls my close.

"Calm down love. You are here with me. I will never let anyone hurt you."

Annetta Hobson

"No that's not it . . . I . . . just . . ."

He leans in and kisses my lips gently. His lips linger on my bottom lip. I taste the cool breeze he exhales as he lifts away from me. He looks me over and there is a hunger in his eyes, one that I do not recognize. He leans in again and the kiss consumes me. I am lost in his passion. He grabs at my tunic I place my hands behind me. He pulls at it once more. He tilts away to look at me again. "Lift your arms over your head."

I oblige. My heart is racing. This feeling is new to me. Our kisses have been little excerpts of stolen romantic moments. Nothing like this. I stretch my hands over my head as if I am reaching for the sky. He slides it over my head and tosses it across the room. My breasts are bound against my chest with a lacey white brassiere. It rises and falls with each breath. I am losing my mind. I don't know what he will do next.

He slides his hand along my arm and tug at them. I know that means I should bring them back down. I rest them on his shoulders.

"We have never had this much time together Chakori. I don't know if I can control myself."

I do not speak. The only thing the leaves my lips are slow ragged breaths. He tilts his head and look at my exposed skin.

"You are such a beauty. I am very lucky to have you. I just do not feel as if I am worthy of such a luxury."

I close my eyes. Suddenly, I feel his breath against my neck followed by his lips. His greedily kisses my body. I feel as if I am being consumed like a meal. He moans. The sound takes me on a ride. My head falls back and he indulges. I feel his hand in my hair. He loosens the bind and my hair spills down my back and prance across my bare skin.

"Elliot." I breathe.

"Yes my love." He says as his hand glides across my back and trails down to my behind. He tugs at my skirt and I instantly realize this has gone too far.

I made a promise from my youth to give myself only to my husband. I will not break that promise. Even now. "We have to stop this has gotten out of hand."

"Please my love. We have only just begun. I want to explore every inch of you. Let's go all the way. You will soon be my bride, so there is no harm."

But he is wrong. I cannot do this it is against everything I believe in. My body is only to be given to my husband on my wedding night. "I really cannot Elliot. This is wrong. Please stop."

He instantly releases me from his embrace. He stands and his pants are bulging. He places his hands over it to hide his arousal. He walks over and retrieves my shirt. He tosses it to me and I quickly dress. He turns away so I cannot see his face.

"I'm so sorry Elliot. I shouldn't have let things get this far."

"Don't worry about it Kori. Just go to sleep love."

I blink quickly to focus on his face. I see the hurt in his blue eyes. I instantly feel sorrow. I never want to hurt the love of my life, but he has to understand. I lay my head on the jackets Elliot folded into pillows for me to rest on. I turn away so I do not have to look at his pained expression. I hear his footsteps. They get closer and closer. The covers rustle and I know Elliot is tightly wound inside the bed he made for the two of us. I hear a shuffle once more.

"Good night my sweet Chakori. I love you with all of my heart." He kisses the back of my head and turns to sleep. Half of the night I stare at the ceiling. I cannot believe I am sleeping in an abandon decaying building. My bed at the mansion is adorned with silk sheets. The comforters are woven with gold embroildery. I have the finest nightwear. Yet I lay in this building awaiting a venture I know nothing about. I have never left the island. In all of my nineteen years, I have not seen what lies behind the line of the ocean. I have never even lay eyes on my enemies land, the island of Jutesh. The sounds that I hear frighten me. The night calls my name. It wants to devour me. But I refuse to turn back. I await the carriage that will carry me to my new home.

I open my eyes. The peeling paint from the cracked ceiling reminds me of my actions. I was hoping to awake in my bed, the dealings of the day before just a dream. But it was all very real. I turn to touch Elliot and he has gone. I sit up. My heart begins to pound. *Did he change his mind? Did my refusal cause him to have second thoughts of our escape?*

I stand. Everything remains in place from the night before. But he is not present. I wish I hadn't left my home. Now I have to return in shame. My father is more than likely dead, made an example of. If you dare cross Khattris you die, simple as that. I must face him alone, my island further torn apart by unrequited love. *How could I expect him to lie beside me and not touch me at all?* I know the island women throw themselves at him daily.

Chronicles of a Betrothed

He is very handsome. His golden brown hair trimmed and fit for a soldier's head. His muscular physique tells it all through his fatigues. He is everything a woman could want and more.

But I am girl, weighed down with tradition. A girl who has been promised to a family full of demons so evil, Mephistopheles could not hold them there. I stand and dust myself off. My eyes began to fill. The fullness in my heart begins to overflow I am choked with regret. *Why do I love this man so?*

Tears stain my cheek I try and wipe them away but it is too late. The salt from my eyes dresses my flushed face as a new ornament. I gather myself and start to collect some of the meal packets. I will need them for my walk back to the mansion. Right now my stomach does not concern me. My heart owns all of my senses. I make my way up to the main floor of the building. The stairs creak beneath my hand crafted shoes. I kick the debris as I slowly walk to the door.

"Where are you going my love? Did I cause you to have second thoughts after last night?"

I do not answer. I run to him and I am lifted off of the dust riddle floor. I wrap my arms around his neck so hard he coughs.

"You are choking me my darling. I need you to loosen your grip. Unless you are trying to kill me." He jokes.

I jump down. The smile has left my face. "I could never hurt you. I love you so much Elliot. It pains me to think of you and the word kill together."

He chuckles. "I am so sorry love. You don't have to worry. I just went to bathe. I don't want you to wake to smelly disgusting man sweat." I take a step back. He is partially dressed his shirt hangs over his shoulder. His body is wet.

"No. You are right. I just thought you had second thoughts and left me. I am handful you know?"

"Yes and one day I will know just how much of a handful you are." He smiles and passes me to enter our temporary abode.

After the dried meat and potato dinner I drink some water out of a small canteen. I stare at it for a moment in between gulps. Yesterday, I was drinking from fine crystal goblets

"What's wrong Chakori?" He asks. I guess my facial expression reveals my mental ramblings.

"Nothing . . . I mean. Why do you ask?"

"You seem troubled. Are you uncomfortable?"

"No Elliot, I am trying to get acquainted with a different life."

"Life is nothing like this in my Country. We are only hiding so you do not get captured by Khattris."

"I understand. I am just letting my mind run wild. I am fine. Really."

Finally I finish my canteen of water, and lie down. I snuggle into the covers and close my eyes. The quiet of the night is unnerving. I close my eyes tighter to concentrate on falling asleep. I hear Elliot tossing and turning. He sighs. I turn to him.

"You can't sleep, can you?"

"No." He huffs.

"Me neither. I guess we are both having trouble sleeping in an abandon court house."

"It's not that." He says as he sits up. "It is killing me to be this close to you and not be able to be with you. I am dying."

I sit up and touch his shoulder. The touch of his bare skin sends shock waves through my body. I jerk my hand back. He smiles.

"I know you feel the same." He says as he slides closer to me.

"It does not matter if I feel the same. We can't until I am your wife."

"What's the difference? We will be married soon."

I sigh. The disparity in his voice concerns me. "We have talked about this for two years. Why must we do it again?"

"Forget about it. Good night Chakori." He slams his head into the roll and closes his eyes. I lay down beside him and fall into a slumber.

Chapter 3

The week we spend in our hide away flies by. My nights are filled with thick tension and desire. When I wake each morning I am startled by his hunger filled eyes watching my every movement. I am afraid I will not be able to resist any longer. This morning is special because it is our last on this island. Tomorrow I leave this life behind. I have to admit I will miss my mother and father. My brother's voice shouting out my name will be nothing but a memory. I will definitely long for the comfort of Yashica. She is the only person who listened to me. She knows my every want and need she is my second mother.

"What was that?" Elliot jumps to his feet. He grabs his shirt and runs to the stairs. He peeks around the corner to get a better look. He looks back at me and I am suddenly alarmed.

"Did you hear that?"

"Hear what . . ."

There is a rustling. Something or someone is in the hall of our hide away.

He runs over to me and pushes me to the broom closet.

I step in and close the door. Suddenly, I hear footsteps. There are a multitude of footsteps. I hear yelling.

"Hear sir! I hear voices in the basement." The stampede stumbles down the stairs. I place my hand over my mouth and sink deeper into the crevice of this broom closet. Fear has stricken me. They have discovered our secret quarters. *Where could Elliot be? Why did he not hide with me?* The voices are getting closer. There is no escape.

"Here are some sleeping bags. They are here."

Oh no, they know I am with someone. They know about Elliot. There is a light that shines on my forehead. It blinds me when I try and focus on it. I move closer to the crack so I can see where they have gone.

"I see something sir!"

I see a man dressed in all black holding a long automatic rifle. He holds it up to his eye as he moves toward a hole in the corner of the room.

"There is someone in there! Come out now! You have been discovered! Give up quietly, and I won't shoot you in your head!"

Elliot crawls out from the hole with his hands held high.

I grip my mouth and squeeze my lips so I will not scream. Tears began to fall uncontrollably from my eyes.

"Where is the girl soldier?" Khattris steps from behind the man yelling. "If you give me the girl you will live. Now tell me where she is now!"

"I don't know what you are talking about? What girl?"

The man dressed in black takes the back of the rifle and smacks him in the face. He falls back and a few more men run and grab Elliot. They bind his hands and stand him back up. Elliot holds his chin up in honor. He has no intension on handing me over to them.

"I know she is here." He lifts my shoes in the air.

Elliot remains true. He doesn't say another word.

"The maid shared all of the details of your little trysts with us. We will find her. And when we do, I will murder her right in front of your face." His eyes grow large. He knows Khattris means it.

"If I tell you where she is will you promise not to hurt her . . . this whole thing was my idea. She is innocent. She is my prisoner."

I gasp. I cannot believe he said that. Surely they will kill him now.

"First soldier, I owe you nothing. And, whether you tell me or not I will discover her where abouts."

"No sir, we were scheduled to board a freight ship tomorrow headed for the United Countries. If you don't find her today she will be gone by morning. And you dare not step foot on that ship. It would be treasonous. My country would storm your island and you would be brought to justice."

Khattris frowns. He knows he is unable to go to war with the UC. He would lose terribly. This is the reason he wars with small islands like mine. Apart from us being his sworn enemies. He needs to build his numbers. He will start with Ghatlan. And then, move to other places with no attachment to the UC. The man with the gun positions it to fire. I sob and my body shudders. I am watching my future husband's potential assassination. He places the tip of the rifle onto Elliot forehead. He lifts it higher so he can see the fear in his eyes.

"Before I kill you young soldier, I must ask. Did you have my son's bride?"

Elliot does not speak.

"ANSWER ME!!!"

Elliot holds his head up in honor. It is horrifying to watch.

"Wait! Here I am. Please do not kill him. He was just doing as I asked. He is protecting me." I burst from the closet and proclaim.

The multitude turns to me. The man with the rifle spins and now I am his target.

"Ah. My dear Chakori." He opens his arms wide and starts towards me. "I was so worried my sweet. Why are you hiding out in this dark dim disgusting place? You are royalty sweetheart act like it." When he reaches me he hugs me as if he missed his darling daughter.

"Oh goodness my dear you smell terrible I'm afraid. We must rectify that immediately." He grabs my hand and starts towards the stairs.

"Before we go darling, please enlighten me. Did this soldier deflower you?"

"Oh no sir. I am an honest girl. I would never break my marital vow. I am still untouched. Only my husband can break my ban."

He smiles and nods.

"What will happen to Elliot? Please do not kill him."

He lets out an evil wail.

"My dear one thing you will learn is to never concern yourself with the affairs of a Monarch. He whisks me up the stairs and the men drag Elliot along. We stand in the grand hall of the once breathtaking structure. Khattris isn't speaking. He rubs his chin as if he is contemplating.

Chronicles of a Betrothed

"Okay this place is secluded. We will be long gone before the UC soldiers discover his body . . ."

"NOOOOOoo!!!" I scream. "Please don't kill him! I will do and go wherever you desire me too. Just do not kill him!" His eyes grow wide.

"Do you love this soldier dear Chakori? Was this an attempt to be with him instead of my son?"

I drop my head. All of the love I feel for Elliot has to be exposed. My love is no longer a secret.

"Yes sir, Monarch Khattris we were to be married when we reached the United Countries."

Elliot rolls his eyes. He seems disappointed I chose to reveal plans to the evilest man alive.

Khattris grabs my arm. "Did you think you could escape and run to the UC? You belong to my son. And, as soon as I prove your purity, you will be delivered to him."

I cringe. I can imagine the evil that exudes from this man passed down a generation, festering in his youth. He is more than likely as evil as his tyrant father.

"Bring him to me." He orders.

"So you planned to kidnap and marry my son's betrothed?"

"I love her more than your son could imagine. No one will ever love her as much as I do." Elliot answers with courage.

Khattris approaches him. His expression is one of disgust with a mixture of admiration. No one has ever stood up to him. He smiles. He stares at Elliot for a moment.

Elliot matches his glare.

"Well, I think we should do something about that." He pulls his suit coat back and reach into what seems like his pocket. As I study closely it is a gun holster. He pulls out a silver shiny handgun and fires right into the side of Elliot's head.

I can't scream. His body tilts to the side. Everything is moving in slow motion. My screams are stifled. They rumble in my belly. I must be dreaming. I close my eyes.

When I open them Elliot, the love of my life is lying in a pool of blood.

"Elliot!!! NOoo!! Please don't die!! I need you!" I cry.

Khattris laughs, grabs a handkerchief from his pocket and wipes the blood that spattered on his hand after he fired. He calmly walks over to me. Everything is moving in a delayed state. Khattris smiles as he approaches me.

My eyes return to Elliot. His eyes are still open. I can't bear the scene that is playing out right in front of me.

Khattris grabs my arm. My head feels light I drift into to darkness.

My eyelids flutter. I try to focus. Everything is blurred. I try to move my arm and it is restrained. I quickly look to my left and I see a beautifully decorated room. I look to my right and I see a tall dark man standing with his arms folded. He is blocking the entrance to the room. I try to speak but my throat is dry. The scratchy sensation feels as if I have swallowed several pins. I try to sit up but my restraints snatch me back to the bed. I glance at the binds and they are made of silk braided ropes. The bed I am confined to has the finest dressing adorning it. It is nothing like the bed at my home. My things are luxury but this place has exceeded anything I own. I scan the room again. There are no windows. But the room is exquisite. I look down at what I am wearing. I have a white satin gown that drapes my body. It is long it covers everything except for my ankles and feet. I look up again and there are magnificent clothes hanging in the open closet. The furniture appears to be very expensive. I look over to the man again.

"Where am I? And who are you?" He does not speak. He stares off. He acts as if I haven't said a word. "I want to know where I am, now!"

His eyes turn to me. He smiles. He clasps his hands together and repositions his stance.

I lay back, my head plops onto the pillow. Tears creep into the corner of my eyes. I hear the door slowly opening.

"Oh yes, our guest is finally awake."

I turn to look and Khattris has entered my luxurious prison.

"Where am I?"

"Oh my dear, you are in the most beautiful and powerful place on earth. You on the island of Jutesh. Happy? You should be. You will experience respect, admiration and enjoy the true finer things. No one can give you what you have here. But, there is one order of business we must handle first." He waves his hand toward the man standing at the door. He walks over to me and unbinds my hands. "Please don't even think about leaving. You are in my home now. And trust me, there is no escape."

I rub my wrist to relieve the burning. I am finally able to sit upright. I sit on the edge of the bed and the door opens once more. A very sexy and seductive woman around the age of 40 walks in. She struts across the room and over to me. She is carrying a black bag in her hands. She is stunning. Her hair is as black as coal. She is slender and tall for a woman. She is dressed strangely. On our island woman do not wear suits. Hers is smoky gray. She has on a plain white dress shirt that a man would wear. It has several buttons from the top unfastened. Her cleavage is exposed. She walks with great confidence.

"This is Dr. Eveleen Agroia. She is our family physician." The woman smiles. "She studied medicine in the United Countries you are so entranced with."

I wrap my arms around myself. "Okay what does that mean?" Suddenly I am painfully reminded that my heart is broken. My beloved Elliot is dead and it is my fault. I will never see the United Countries now or ever. Sadness engulfs me. I look to the floor and cover my eyes.

"Don't be afraid. I am very gentle. I was taught well. I studied in the UC for the first 10 years of my career. I will not hurt you."

I wipe the tears from my eyes. "How is it over there?"

She smirks. "It is as any other place. None is as beautiful as Jutesh. Even the United Countries have no land that could compare to the beauty of this island. Khattris has given you the precious gift, a life free from war. As a bonus, you get to marry my wonderfully handsome godson. Well, if you pass this exam."

"I will leave you two alone Eve. I will return shortly." He presses his lips together.

Neither frown nor smile takes shape. He exits the room and the man that is guarding me leaves also.

She steps closer. I jerk away in fear. "Relax Chakori. I assume no one has ever handled you in this manner before?"

"No ma'am. I am untouched."

"Well, we will see." She opens her bag and pulls out a pair of surgical gloves. She slides them on. She grabs a silver device from the bag and approaches me.

"I am afraid. What does that do?"

"Again Chakori, you must relax. First, I would like you to remove your underwear."

I gasp. I have never been totally naked in front of anyone since I have been an adult. I hesitate.

"I really do not want to do this Dr…"

"My name is Eveleen. But you may call me Eve. You have no choice in the matter. You must remove your underwear or he will send one his goons to do it for you. I am extending you a courtesy. I have given you the option of being alone with me. It wasn't easy but he trusts me. He wanted to watch. He would have had his head right where I work. Is that what you want?"

"No!' I exclaim totally mortified. I stand and remove my underwear. "Do you know how long I have been here? And, who dressed me?"

She steps toward me and place a hand on my shoulder as I sit.

"He has several servants, motherly ones. One of them probably. And, as far as I know, you have been here for two days. I was told you were very upset. So I have been keeping you sedated."

"Oh no! My parents must be insane with worry."

"No, they are aware of your where abouts. I actually know your parents. I have been allowed on your island several times over the years. I have attended some of the wounded soldiers. I am a doctor so we have to remain neutral in the wake of war."

I nod. I have never seen this woman before. She has visited my home and I had no knowledge of it. I feel betrayed. What else did I not know? My father was full of lies. I slide onto the bed. I place my head on the pillow and close my eyes.

She touches my thigh and I begin to shiver. I have never been touched by a man. And now, this woman, whom I do not know, is about to enter in my inner most sacred crevices.

"Open your legs and prop them up. I need your feet planted firmly though."

I am shaking. I can't control it. I place my hands on my knees to try and steady them but it does not help.

She lifts her device in the air so I can see it. "I am going to use this to get a look inside you. First, I will insert my fingers to examine you."

She places the device beside me. It rolls and rests on my leg. The metal is cold, I jump.

"Try to relax. This will go much quicker if you just relax."

She inserts her fingers. She pushes them deep inside me. I close my eyes. I cannot believe what is happening. Elliot never got to be with me. But this stranger is delving into my most treasured area.

"Let your knees fall apart Chakori. Relax them as they fall."

I try to oblige but the thoughts flood my mind. Elliot should have been the person to first explore my tunnels. But it is too late. Tears overtake me. Soon I am sobbing.

"Chakori." She sighs. "You are over thinking this. It is only an exam. I am being gentle aren't I?"

"Yes ma'am." I sob. "But I wanted my husband to be the first to enter. That is ruined forever."

Sympathy replaces her intolerance. "I understand. I didn't think of that. I am almost done." She removes her fingers and crouches. She looks at my womanhood. She sits on the bed and grabs the device.

"This should be warm now since it rested against your body. I am going to insert it now okay?"

I nod. I close my eyes to brace myself. The pressure is bearable. She slides it in gently. I grab the covers and clinch my teeth. She does what she came to do.

"All done. See it wasn't that bad was it?"

I shake my head. I hated every moment of it. I am relieved it is finally over. She stands and walks over to the door and knocks.

Khattris rushes in.

"Well, Eve." He says breathlessly.

"She is definitely untouched Pavan. I assure you. No man has ever even touched her there."

"Are you sure Eve?"

She frowns. "I am absolutely positive. This was by far the worst and most uncomfortable exam I have ever given. Girls ten years her youth is not as nervous. I am very confident in my findings."

"Great we will celebrate! Surely, you will join us?"

"Of course. I will not miss the introduction of Daler's new bride to be." She turns and extends a wide smile. "It was very nice to meet you Chakori Desai of Ghatlan."

"Soon to be Chakori Khattris of Jutesh." Monarch Khattris interrupts.

"Of course. When is the celebration Pavan?"

"I am thinking tomorrow night. I can put everything together. But I will let my wife handle it all. She loves parties." The smile is wiped clean from her face at the mention of his wife.

"How is Surina? Is she well?" she says in a sarcastic tone.

"She is fine Eveleen. Why do you ask?" he presses through his teeth.

"I am just concerned for her health. You are always promising to talk to her about that. But it seems you never get to. It is just a shame. That's all."

"Are you threatening me? I would hate for you to overstep your boundaries and cause an early retirement. Jai is dying, I mean dying to replace you."

She laughs. Replace me if you like. If I disappear my friends in the United Countries will . . ."

He snatches her arm.

"Pack you instruments away now!"

She swallows hard. As she packs her things she gives me a nervous smirk. "Good luck my dear you will need it here."

She picks up her medical bag from the bed and Khattris drags her from the room.

Chapter 4

I am left utterly confused of what just occurred. I stand and slide into my underwear. I pull my gown down and look around the room. I walk over to the closet. I run my hands along the line of garments. Each one is neatly pressed. I push them aside one by one. I love the wardrobe but it changes nothing. I still hate this place and the man it belongs to. I hear the door open. The gorilla who is assigned to watch me has returned. I turn back to my exploration of my new wardrobe. I step into the closet and behind the clothes there is a large armoire with double doors elegantly carved. I run my fingers along the markings. They are like nothing I have ever seen. I daydream of what life would be like if I accept my fate. *Will I be allowed to come and go as I please? Or will I be a prisoner no matter what I do?*

"Mistress?"

I quickly turn startled by a deep voice.

"Are you hungry? I am told you have not eaten in days."

I grab my stomach. He is correct. I can't remember what I ate last. I think and the memory of Elliot and I eating dried meat from packages cause me to cringe. Suddenly my brain has taken control of my stomach and it starts to grumble, loud.

Annetta Hobson

"I assume that is a yes?"

I nod. "I would like to eat. Would you be so kind as to go and fetch me a meal?"

"I would like to formally introduce myself I am Emund. I am from the hot country. It is a continent in the United Countries. I came here years ago and I loved it. It is most gorgeous."

"Oh, did you know any of the soldiers aiding Ghatlan?"

"I am afraid I do not. But would you please go bath and dress? I will wait in the hall." He turns to leave and I touch his back. He is stunned by my touch he grabs my hand.

"Never touch the guards Mistress. You are not allowed to touch any man here. Is that clear?"

"Y. . . Y . . . Yes. I apologize." I blink. I am left completely bewildered. I rush to my private bathroom to bathe. It is a perfectly decorated as well. *How long will I be in this room and why are there so many personal things of mine in here? Will I be separated from his family for the duration of a year? Or will I get to mingle and get to know them?* I take a bath and dry myself off. I stop at the mirror on my way out of the bathroom. I have never examined my own body. I look at my perky breast. They bounce when I move. My eyes travel down to my stomach. I have a small mole beside my navel I only notice it when I am sliding on my underwear. My center is covered in curly reddish brown hair like the hair on my head. I look at my hips and my thighs and I know they are made for carrying babies. I rub my hands across my stomach. My body is very beautiful. I have never studied it in this manner. I part my legs and I see my womanhood. It is a natural sight, well-shaped. I am sure Elliot would have loved to touch it before he was brutally murdered. But he will never get to be with me. Never having the chance to dive in. I touch it and the sensation reminds me of the night he kissed me. I close my eyes and let my fingers explore. It felt different then when the doctor examined me. The sensation was pleasurable. I moan at the feeling I am unleashing on my body. I fall against the door and rub my fingers around. The bulb in the center is the most sensitive. That must be the pleasure center. Oh how I would have loved to let Elliot have me. I take my fingers and slide them across my button. It sends my head into a whirl. Suddenly, I hear the door of my room open. My eyes pop open and I grab my towel to cover myself.

"I am not dressed! I will be ready in a moment." I peek around the corner and I see a man standing beside my bed. "Sir, I am not dressed, can you please leave."

He turns around and I see his face. It is a handsome face. He is dressed in a white shirt and black slacks. He has on very grand looking shoes. He smiles when he sees my face.

"Chakori. You're quite a beauty. I will leave now but I will be back."

I frown. "Who are you?"

He smirks and opens the door. Before he steps out he speaks. "Just get dressed. If I stay in this room I will want to see more than just your naked shoulder."

I look at my body and cover my mouth. He closes the door behind him and I am intrigued by him. *Who was that? And, why was he in my room?* He has dark colored short wavy hair. He had a nicely trimmed mustache with a goatee to match. His dark features reminded me of . . . Khattris! *That has to be his son! Oh no, he is gorgeous! I did not know I would be so attracted to him.*

Annetta Hobson

Maybe it is because I was touching myself when he entered but I am overwhelmed by his handsome face and grand stature. I quickly run to my closet and find something to wear. Everything is elaborate. *I do not think a gown is necessary for a dinner for one. But I guess he just wants me to wear dresses.* So I try to find the least grand gown and put it on. It is gray with silver lining. It has a tight bodice and is fitted to my body. I slide on some silver heels to complete the look. I sit in the bed and wait for my meal. I do not know the time so I assume I am eating dinner.

About an hour passes and I am growing tired of waiting. I stand and walk to the door. I turn the knob and it is locked, of course. I stomp my beautifully dressed self-back to the bed and lie on my stomach. I dangle the shoe on the tips of my toes. Before I kick it off, I hear the door open. *It is Khattris son again?* My heart races with expectation. I am afraid to turn around. I want it to be him but I instantly feel guilty. *These are the people who killed my love. I should hate him, and I will.* I jerk around. "Finally! I am starving. I have been dressed for a while Emund!"

"I apologize Mistress. I was told you were indisposed. And to give you about an hour."

"Indisposed? How? It took me minutes to dress."

Emund's dark skin flushes.

Could Khattris son been aware of what I was doing? Did he hear my moans? My skin flushes and our expressions match one another. "Nevermind. Where is my dinner?"

"Mistress you are not eating in here. You have been summoned to eat with the parents of your husband to be."

"Oh." I inhale. "I assumed I was a prisoner. I did not think I would be leaving the room."

Chronicles of a Betrothed

Emund begins to speak but is silenced.

"You were never a prisoner Chakori. I just wanted to make sure you were not lying to me my dear." Khattris enters.

"Then why is my door locked?"

"So you will not get any ideas. I can't have you abandoning my son. I really like you. I don't want to have to hurt you. Your father would not be happy about that. Right?"

I nod. This man is pure evil. His smile is beautiful, much like his son. But it is the smile of a devil.

"Of course, Monarch Khattris. I would not want to upset you either."

"Oh, good girl. You catch on fast. Tonight will be your last night in this room. I will have it moved to the east wing with the families. But if you ever try to escape, I will have your little brother tortured and killed before you reach the water of my fine island. Understand?"

Fear riddles me. He is worst then I could ever imagine. My brother is six. *How could anyone hurt a child?* I believe this man have and will. *I hate him and I will never love his son. All of my hatred will be geared toward this family. I swear this.* I walk down the long hall. I turn when he turns. I follow his every step.

Emund matches my stride.

My hands are clutched firmly in front of me. I walk with ease. My heart is pounding but I make no reference to it. I look as cool as the evening breeze beside the water. We walk down a flight of stairs. The mansion is fascinating. My mother was not exaggerating. They have money, and lots of it. I can tell that each statue I pass is made of materials not found here. They must be imported. My father had opportunities to trade with the United

Annetta Hobson

Countries but he refused. He did not want them to try and control him. Our justice was our own. The moment we started to trade with them we would have lost our island's freedom. My father paid for the soldiers. Our natural resources were worth a lot to them so there were some negotiations that left us with no obligation to them. But it looks like Khattris deals directly with them. Which leads me to believe *he is afraid of their potential interference?* That is probably why he does not want Eveleen speaking with them.

"Okay darling here we are."

I step into a dining room like no other. It is elegantly designed. The tables and chairs are made of all natural stones. Exquisite art adorns the walls.

"Your home is breathtaking."

"This is your home now too. So reference as such."

"Yes sir."

He takes his hand and places it on my back. "This is my lovely wife and your soon to be mother, Surina."

I nod.

"These are my equally as beautiful daughters Jasmine and Jasleen. There are close to your age Chakori. Maybe you can become close. Jasmine is 20 and Jasleen is 17."

"Very nice to meet you." I say completely formal. I was unaware of his daughters. *I wonder if he will marry them off one day as my father did me.* They both stand and prance over to me. They simultaneously hug me and I am smothered. They finally release me and I am invited to sit by their mother. All of them have the same look. The girls are a mixture of their mother who has silky brown long hair that hangs down her back. She has

Chronicles of a Betrothed

slanted eyes and full lips. She is medium build but not considered overweight.

"Hello Chakori. I know this is different for you but we will take very good care of you. Is there anything you want to know?"

I sit in my seat and Emund is quickly behind me sliding my chair underneath the table.

"What is your son's name and how old is he?"

She smiles. "Ahhh you are interested in your betrothed. I see. Well, he is 24 years old. His name is Daler Khattris." She turns to her husband. "Pavan you did not inform her of her future husband's name?"

He shakes his head and waves over the staff.

They start to bring a slew of food.

Everything I could have imagined is being set in front of me. I feel like a vagrant. My stomach is so empty.

"He is a very handsome young man. I am sure you will be the most hated young woman in Jutesh. He looks a lot like Pavan. You are very lucky. Daler refuses to marry any woman on the island. He all but insisted he have you today. I do not know what changed. Because when his father announced his plan he almost started an ingrown war. He must have been hearing ramblings of your uncanny beauty around the mansion."

I smile. "When do I get to meet him?"

"Oh you cannot meet him until the announcement is made at the party we have set for tomorrow."

"Oh I see. I am patient. I don't mind."

Her expression changes. "I heard about your soldier. I am very sorry."

Khattris sends her a death stare.

"Calm down Pavan. We are family here it will not leave this room. I just want to express my sympathy."

"Thank you very much. I will miss him dearly. I have never known love like his and now I guess I never will again."

"Nonsense. I think Daler will fall madly in love when he gets to know you, much like Pavan and I."

He frowns at her suggestion.

"Okay you have done that. Now let's eat."

We join hands and bow our heads. Then we eat. I wolf the food down until I am bursting at the seams. When I look up from my plate the Khattris daughters are staring at me. I wipe my mouth. "I apologize I have not eaten in a few days." They accept my explanation and ask their father if it's okay to retire.

I sit at the grand dining table silent. I watch as Monarch Khattris and his wife talk. They converse as if I am no longer present.

Suddenly Surina stands. "I am very sorry Chakori but I must retire. I have a long day ahead of me tomorrow. Will you excuse me?"

I stand. "Of course."

She walks over to me and hugs me. She kisses my cheek softly. "Goodnight sweet Chakori."

And I watch as she retires for the evening. I sit back into my chair.

Monarch Khattris stands.

"I also must leave you. But remember my warning. I will not chase you. I will just follow through on my warning. Emund will take you to your new room. It is bigger and better than the one you were in."

Chronicles of a Betrothed

"Thank you sir. I will not defy you. I am grateful for your kindness."

"Excellent. Have a good evening Chakori. Your things are waiting for you in the new room. I had them moved while we dined."

I bow my head as he stands. The fear this man exudes is wrenching. I believe he would kill my brother so I will never leave here. I will stay and endure a loveless marriage for as long as I and Daler live.

"Mistress Chakori." A sweet voice chimes. I turn and a small petite woman is speaking.

"Yes."

"Would you like desert?"

"Yes, I would love desert."

She disappears through the doors and when she returns she is carrying a cake that seems too good to be real. I follow the cake with my eyes until she places it in front of me. I dig in. The taste is heavenly, why had I never had cake like this in Ghatlan.

"This cake tastes sinful, I love the way it dances on my tongue."

"Oh, so first, you enjoy long baths, secret bathroom trysts and now you love things that dance on your tongue. I am starting to wonder about my innocent betrothed. You are not as innocent as my father says."

I turn around. Oh no there he is again, confirming my suspicions. I am totally embarrassed. He knows about my first erotic feeling. He was there as I pleasured myself. I guess it is not all bad. He will be my husband.

He walks calmly toward me. I am frozen. I do not say a word. He stops beside and places his fists on the table.

"So you are Chakori." He surveys me.

I feel like art put out for display.

He slowly begins to walk circling behind me. He does not take his eyes off of me.

I can feel the burn he is radiating.

"You are lovely I must say. My father did not exaggerate your beauty. I am really taken back." He grabs my bound hair. It tumbles down and splashes around my shoulders.

"Our women do not bind their hair. They wear it how they please. Does it please you to wear it this way?"

"Uh… No sir… I"

He chuckles.

"You are nervous? Why? Is it because I interrupted you earlier? Don't worry I won't tell my father. As a matter of fact," he leans close to my ear and whispers. "I will show how it is really done, my young bride to be. I am very skilled with my fingers. You will definitely get to finish." He leans back and begins to walk. He gets to the other side of me and stops. He stares and I am afraid to look.

My breathing is picking up. I am so nervous my entire body is quivering.

"Why do you squirm? I have not touched you yet?"

I am paralyzed with fear. Why can't I move?

"Answer me Chakori." He whispers.

"I don't know. I guess I am just afraid. I do not know what to expect." He giggles.

I amuse him.

"We are not supposed to be fraternizing are we? Your mother said . . ."

"I do as I please. She does not control me. Besides I was dying to see the hag my father was forcing me to marry."

I gasp. *He thought I was a hag*!

"Were you not curious about me?"

"No, after Ell . . . I mean I just except the fate that has been bestowed upon me."

"Well, just for reference, I like what I see. I can't wait to see if I like how you feel. I haven't had a virgin in a very long time." He laughs and moves closer. He bends and his face is directly in front of mine. I can feel his breath on my cheek. I close my eyes. "Why do you close your eyes? I am a sight you surely want to see."

He is arrogant. And, he has every right to be. He is stunning. I am mourning Elliot but his appearance has caught my attention.

"Daler sir."

He stands up straight and spins to greet whomever is summoning him.

"Yes."

"Your father needs you now!!" A man says clearing his throat as he hurries in our direction.

"I will be there shortly."

The man eyes cut to me.

I am breathing so rapidly surely he suspects something has occurred. His eyes leave me and he exits the room.

"I guess I will continue this at a later time." He leans close to me again and his lips graze my cheek. "Your smell is exhilarating. Ummm." He moans. Suddenly he stands and struts from the room. He straightens his jacket as he leaves. I am left wallowing in angst.

Chapter 5

"I need to go to the restroom Emund. Where is it?"

He points. "Go down that hall and turn left you should see it." I slide my chair back and stand. I straighten my gown and walks slowly to the door. I walk down the hall and I cannot find the bathroom. I search relentlessly and there is no bathroom in sight. I knock on doors but there is no answer. This home is intimidating. My home was large but this mansion reminds me of the castles my father read of hundreds and hundreds of years ago. I have gone too far. I hear the muffled sounds of someone arguing. I step towards the stairwell. I take a step down and the sound becomes clear. I step down to get a little closer. The voices are still not clear enough for me to hear the conversation. I take off my heels and quietly tip down the stairs. There is a dungeon type basement at the foot of the stairs. I can hear the voices much clearer. I walk toward the yelling.

"You dare threaten me! Are you insane Eve? Just because are my lover does not mean you have any leverage! And, you dare threaten the First Lady's life! She is the mother of my children."

Annetta Hobson

"So am I, but you have taken my child from me. I did not even get to see his face. It is not fair. You say I am the one you love, yet you hide me and praise her."

"Look, you are my father's mistress. And, you must learn your place!" I creep closer and peek into the room. I look behind me to make sure I am not discovered. I nudge at the door and it budges a little, just enough for me to see. A tall muscular man drags a younger man inside of the room. The man is sniveling. His hands are bound and he has a mask over his eyes.

"No! What are you doing with my brother?"

Daler smiles. "I am going to show you your position."

"Please, I promise I will never speak of her again. Do not hurt him. He has a family! His wife carries his child."

Khattris walks over to the man. His nose is running and he is begging to be let go. Daler follows his father. He reaches the man and rips off his blind fold.

"Here is you sister. Thank her for you demise." He pulls a huge jagged edged knife from a nearby table and plunges into his chest. He twists it and the man screams in pain. I grab my mouth to stifle my scream. *This man is as evil as his father.* Tears run down my cheeks and over my hand. The doctor screams out. She drops her head and sobs. The man falls limp and the tall man drags him away. The trail of blood is stained in my mind as I run up the stairs. I run so fast I drop my shoe. I stop to pick it up and I spot Emund coming for me.

"Did you find the rest room Mistress?"

"No Emund just take me to my room." I say out of breath. I nearly collapse from horror.

Chronicles of a Betrothed

He grabs me and assists me to the other side of the mansion and up the stairs to my quarters. "Are you okay?"

"I am fine Emund. I guess I just have had a long week. I need rest nothing more."

I get to the door and he pushes it open. The room is not what I expected. It is indescribable. I am in hell but it looks stunning. I walk over to the bed and I have a bit of technology in this room. Ghatlan did not have most technology. When the United Countries combined everything changed. The Continents that once stood alone where apart of governing nations. They no longer had the right to crown king or queens. The President of the old States had taken over most of the world. The islands outside of the covenant remained free. The seclusion of our lands made us virtually invisible until about 50 years ago. Some explorers were flying the aircrafts over Jutesh and we were discovered shortly thereafter. They tried to get our land to connect under the one world monarchy but our grandfathers remained steadfast. And we are one of the few lands who remain independent from the UC. The new millennium did not bring about the change they had hoped. Technology slowed but is still vital. It is just more frequently used in the UC.

I sit on the bed. I examine my surroundings. I reflect on my meeting with Daler Khattris. *He is as evil as his father. I do not want to marry him. He is a murderer. And, I have to actually lay with him one day.* My stomach turns at the thought. *He may want to kill me.* Who will come to my rescue? I am a stranger in this land and I have no one. I stand and walk over to the bathroom door. I stare in the mirror. I really miss Elliot. His life was taken because of me. *I should not have agreed to leave with him and he* would be alive. *I at least should have made love to my beloved.* I would have probably been killed for the betrayal but I would've experienced real love. Now, I am bound to of life of malice and greed. I will never know what it feels like to make love.

The next morning I awake and the heaviness on my heart is constricting. My love for Elliot haunts me. I cannot believe I am living with the people responsible for his death. I sit up and look over to a window that is reflecting light. I stand and quickly go over to it. I open the window and look at out of. The scenery from this room is gorgeous. I watch the palm trees sway with the morning breeze. The sun beautifully reflects off of the ocean. It is nothing like Ghatlan. *How can our islands be so close and yet look like they are worlds apart?* I am mesmerized by the view. My heart grieves as I enjoy this island run by a madman. The houses surrounding the mansion match its grand architecture. I am ripped from my thoughts when I am interrupted by a knock at my door. "Yes?" I say as I turn.

"Hello. I was hoping you would accompany me to breakfast." Jasleen says as she enters.

"Oh, of course. I was just admiring the view. This island has great beauty. I see why your family loves it so."

"I guess." She curls her lip at the side as she speaks.

"So I have to get dressed but I should be ready in about 20 minutes." I expect her to leave but she lingers. I walk over to the closet and sift through the fine array of garments. I try and find something that is not fit for a gala. As a slide the clothes along the rack she speaks again.

"Chakori?"

"Yes." I turn to face her. "What is it Jasleen?"

Chronicles of a Betrothed

She clinches her hands together and begins to rub them.

"I am afraid for you. My family is very dysfunctional. Especially, my brother."

I gasp. The sound of her voice is starting to fade. I have been trying to remain calm. But her concern has caused my strength to unravel. She attempts to sit on the edge of the huge bed. She has to jump up on it to sit.

"Why do you say that?" I say trying to steady my voice.

"Please do not pretend to not know about my family. We are sworn enemies from birth."

"No, I am aware of that. I just don't understand your concern for me."

"You are very pretty Chakori."

"Thank you?" I return in confusion.

"You have not met Daler yet. He is very charming. But he is the splitting image of my father. And, not just his looks. My father is mad. He has no heart. I am surprise my mother loves him so much. I despise them both."

I walk over to the bed and sit beside her. "You despise your father and brother, why?"

"I don't know about you, but murdering and torturing people are not something you want to be known for. The people here hate us. They fear them so they respect us. I may have to go away to have a husband that will touch me. "

"Isn't that a task your father must be concerned about?"

"Yes. But if we find love on our own we will be allowed to marry whom we desire. Only Daler's mate is chosen. He is the eldest and the only son. So Jasmine and I are off the hook."

"Does Jasmine have a husband?"

"No. She wants to go to the United Countries for school. One of the professors at the college is from there and believes Jasmine needs to explore the world before she becomes a Justice over our main Court. Maybe she will find a husband there and not return."

"I see. Do you have several courts here?"

"Yes, we have 12. Father thought if the people had more than one court they would be more open to the belief in them. It really worked too. The people of this island believe they will actually receive fair and lawful decisions in these courts. But my father is the final judge he decides what will be, no one else. Jasmine wants to take the main court because she believes father will let her decisions stand. But I do not."

I am shocked and in awe with the daughters of Khattris. They are nothing like their father. Maybe their mother is such a saint she penetrated the heinous blood that flows through the veins of their children. I look at the door. My mind starts to race. *Why is she afraid for me? What will he do to me? I have to know. So why don't I just ask?* "Jasleen. What is it that concerns you about Daler and I?"

She sighs. She grabs my hand and looks directly into my eyes. "My father loves my mother. But if she crosses the line . . . well if she meddles in the affairs of the land he," a grim look crosses her face. Her eyes trail off, she is no longer in this room. When she snaps back she continues. "He used to beat my mother, terribly beat her. I did not think she would live through it sometimes. I hate him for that. But I try to forget. It has been many years since he last abused her. She has learned to stay out of the politics of this land. And she does not meddle in his personal affairs either."

Chronicles of a Betrothed

I am utterly and totally disgusted with Monarch Pavan. He is the worst person alive. I am sure there are rulers in the past that were bad. But this man is the unadulterated epitome of the word evil. And I have been assured by my own accounts and now Jasleen's, that he is the same. What will I do? I am going to marry a man that is horribly immoral. I want to die.

"Well, I will leave you alone so you can dress for breakfast. Please remember what I have shared with you Chakori. Your father made a grave mistake trusting mine. I pray you and I grow close." She stands and walks over to the door. Before she opens it she takes one more look at me and leaves.

I am left alone with my thoughts. I sit on the bed sure as ever. I don't want to be here. But if I break away he will surely kill my brother. I am stuck in this hell with no chance of escaping. I go over to the closet and select a blue dress. It is not fit for breakfast. None of the things in this closet is fit for a quiet breakfast. I bathe and dress. I look in the full length mirror on the far corner wall. My reflection is one of a princess, which is what I am in technical terms. *I am sad that my father has thrown me literally to the wolves.* I take a deep breath and head for the door. I turn the knob and open it.

There is Emund standing there waiting.

"Good morning Mistress."

"Good Morning Emund. How are you?"

He nods.

I am especially nervous. Today, is the start of complete interactions with my husband to be. I don't know how I will react towards him after witnessing him plunge a knife deep into a man's chest. I cringe at the thought. *Murder has never been so real to me. And, thanks to my betrothed, I am introduced to it in living color.* I slowly walk to the dining area from the night before. As I approach the entrance my heart beats so loud it feels as if it is inside of my ears. Khattris is very scary. I do not want to make him angry, so I must mind my words. I step into the room and everyone is present. Jasleen smiles as I walk toward the table.

"Here Chakori, sit beside Me." she says.

I hurry to the seat next to her. I sit and Emund slides me in.

"Good morning Chakori. How do you like your new room?" Khattris asks.

I stuttered trying to speak to fast. "FFF...fine. It is lovely."

The sight of him sends my mind into a frenzy. I try to calm down but the murders I witnessed rings in my head. *This monster killed Elliot, and then they murdered the doctor's brother.* The food arrives and I stuff my mouth so I will not be asked anything else.

"Whoa! You need to slow down Chakori." Jasleen adds.

I swallow my food and drink from the crystal glass. I wipe my mouth with the napkin and try to calm myself once more.

"Chakori." Khattris says as he wipes his mouth. "My son will not be attracted to you if you conduct yourself that way in his presence. Did your father not tell me you were properly trained? Do the women on your island eat like swine? Look around you. My women eat like proper women of dictatorship. You are in the presence of greatness. Conduct yourself accordingly. Or I will have to show you. And trust me, you will not like it. I promise you that."

I am paralyzed with fear. *Why did I do that? I was not trying to act out. I was trying to calm myself.* I panic. I remember when he hit me in my father's office. *I had never been struck before. And I never want to again.* "I am very sorry sir. It will never happen again, especially because I want your son to be impressed with me. I assure you that it won't happen again. Please accept my humble apology."

He smiles. His eyes wrinkle at the corner. The thought he was probably the most handsome man I had ever met disturbed me. I hated they were such beautiful people on the outside. I know that I am going to detest the touch of his son but I knew having children with him was in my future.

"I know you will be ready. I want you to go out today and find attire for this evening. This is the single most important evening in history. I want you to be breathtaking. My son has to be absolutely taken by you. I will have my staff come in and help you prepare. They will take care of how you will bathe, your hair and they will dress you. Jasmine and Jasleen will accompany you. I hope you enjoy the scenery. Our island has great sights."

Chapter 6

"This is our garment store. All of our fine dresses come from here." Jasmine points as we turn onto a lovely block of merchants.

The storefronts are beautifully built. The architecture once again impresses me. "What craftsman designed your buildings? On Ghatlan our buildings do not have as much character."

"Our building designer is from the United Countries. Many of their resources are brought here for us to partake. Before that our island probably looked much like yours."

I turn to glance at Jasleen. She stares from the window with sadness. I touch her hand and she takes a deep breath.

"What is it?" I ask. She does not respond. I look to Jasmine and she is frowning.

"She just wants too much. Father is not going to bend. He is a Monarch he doesn't have to."

Suddenly, I am confused. Jasleen did not disclose any plans that she has. What could Jasmine be referring to?

"Shut up Jasmine! You do not know anything about me. All you care about is that you will be leaving soon. You will be in the comfort of the United Countries. Out of father's reach. You don't even have to return if that is your desire. I should be going not you!"

"You are a fool Jasleen. Father will never trust you to go to the UC. Daler and I are trustworthy. We want what's best for Jutesh. You want what is best for you!"

"I want to be free of this horrible family. Father has the nerve to subject another person to this misery. I feel for Chakori. She has no idea what is in store. She has no idea of the treacherous future that lies ahead."

"Silence Jasleen! Or I will tell father of your ramblings. You are scaring her. Look at the fear in her eyes."

They both turn to me. I blink so the fear that consumes me isn't evident. *They have no idea what I know. What I have witnessed. And I will never speak of it.*

The car stops. Jasmine jumps from the vehicle and stomps into the building. Jasleen turns to me and begin to speak.

"Jasmine is blinded. She never saw the bruises father gave mother. She does not know of Daler's evil ventures. She is under the impression that people fear them only because of their stature. She is a fool. And I take back everything I said about her. Do not trust her either."

We step from the vehicle. I survey the area. This island is even grander in person. The sun shines diligently. The trees sway in a dancing rhythm. I am taken by the beauty of a place where I am forced to live. I can't help but admire it, even though it is my prison. I step inside of the store and the gowns are more elegant than all of the gowns in my closet. I have never worn such mesmerizing fabrics. I think of the seamstresses who made my clothes and feel cheated somehow.

Chronicles of a Betrothed

The children of Jutesh live with the ability to leave their home to shop, dine, party and play. While on the island of Ghatlan we had to be escorted by soldiers from far away. If I wanted to go outside for a breath of fresh air there had to be some soldier tailing me. Our strategies did not faze Khattris. The counter attacks did not even reach the main land. It is unbelievable. The frequented places on my island are destroyed. These sit here with no evidence of the terror ever being unleashed. I rub my forehead and study my surroundings.

"Chakori? Do you see anything that you like?" Jasleen asks. I quickly shake from my envious thoughts.

"Oh let's see . . . there are so many. I don't know which one to choose."

Jasmine paces. Her patience is wearing thin.

"Look Daler loves the color blue. He would like you in this." She points to a blue and silver gown. It is separate from the others.

"That would be fine. I will take it."

Jasmine grabs the dress and the woman attending the store takes it in the back. When she returns it is wrapped in a garment bag.

I am whisked to the car and back to the mansion. I am escorted back to my room by Emund. *When I am married to Daler I wonder if Emund will still be my shadow.* I walk into my room and pull off my shoes. I slip out of the dress I am wearing and toss it onto the bed. I walk back over to the door and lock it. Since I have changed rooms, I have control over who comes and goes. I walk towards the bathroom massaging my neck. The sisters are quite a handful to deal with. I had friends but I was not around other women my age often. I walk to the bathroom and the door is closed. I turn the knob and I hear the water running. I step back and think. *Did I leave the water on?* I turn the knob and the door opens. I push it and I gasp. Daler is standing in the middle of the bathroom with a towel on.

I try to cover my bra with my hands. His eyes travel up and down my body. I turn to run and get a robe but he grabs me.

"Where are you going?" My heart starts to beat. The pace speeds as he draws me near.

"I need to put something on sir. I am sorry for being inappropriate. I didn't know you were in here." I try to pull free but he will not release me.

"Why are you trying to get free? I just want to talk to you. I wanted to be alone. So I decided to come take a shower in here. It was my understanding you would be out all evening. Are you uncomfortable with my nudity?"

I gulp. My heart will not quiet. I am shuddering at his touch. I don't know if it is from the fact that he is a murdering tyrant's son or that he is standing in my room wet from a shower. The way his hair is lying down on his head, it drips down his muscular back. With every movement he flexes. I don't want to but I find myself intrigued by him. He looks very delectable. I know it's wrong. These people killed Elliot and there is no way to remedy that. "Are you going to answer? I hate asking questions twice."

"I apologize sir. I am very uncomfortable with your nudity. It is not appropriate. Monarch Khattris says . . ."

He releases my arm and I cross them. He rubs his hands through his wet hair. He tightens the towel and walks from the bathroom.

I follow him with my eyes only.

Chronicles of a Betrothed

He sits on the bed, opens his legs and smiles.

I step out and walk slowly to the closet. As I walk my eyes rest on his inner thigh. I have never seen a man virtually naked. I am very distracted.

"Do you like what you see Chakori?"

I shake my head realizing that he is doing this on purpose.

"What are you referring to sir?"

I reach the closet and grab my robe. Before I can slide it on he grabs it and tosses it across the room. Now I am afraid. I am unaware of his intensions. He places his hands on my bare hips and pulls my midsection towards him.

"If someone were to catch us I would surely die sir. And, I do not want to die."

He smirks.

"I would not allow it. You are mine now. And not even my father can take you away from me. They decided to make me marry you. And I have never wanted to marry any woman. The thousands of women on this island have been presented to me, young and old. I have had many of them for the sake of pleasuring myself. My father grew tired which is no concern to me. But when I heard you had finally arrived I had to see the woman who ran away from marrying the most powerful eligible heir around."

"I . . . I am so sorry I ran." I stutter "I was already prepared to marry someone else. Someone I loved."

"Ahh yes, how did that work out for you? Oh, he is dead. Right?"

I gasp at his abrasiveness. I want to respond but the wrong words could lead to my expedited death.

Annetta Hobson

"Yes, he is dead."

"Do not fret young Chakori. Love is truly overrated. Your soldier is dead. But now you have wealth and unlimited resources. Trust me when I say you are better off. What were you going to do? Try and rebuild the ruins of Ghatlan? Raise your children with the little you know as wealth? My darling you have been blessed with an abundance of wealth. I would be offended by your choice but I am much too arrogant for that."

"I am here now. I embrace my fate. I will adhere to the treaty. You will never have to worry about me fleeing. I treasure my life. And now I know that this is something I have to do. I will be yours and yours only." I look to my feet. The more I speak the closer he gets. He is now breathing into my hair. The heat from his breath moves me. I want to loathe him. But with each meeting I am curious. This man is loved by many women, they desire him. Yet here I am with him and it is the last place I want to be. I think?

"Chakori." He whispers. "Look at me."

I slowly bring my eyes to meet his. That hunger I recognized in Elliot is burning through me.

"You belong to me now. And, I will do whatever I want with you."

His glare paralyzes me. I do not move. He captures my jaw between his fingers and brings my lips to his. He leans down to me. His lips touch mine and it is electrifying. Magnetic jolts explode through my body. He grabs my hands clinched to my thighs and wraps them around his neck.

Suddenly, I am lost in this mad man's embrace and I do not want to let go.

Chronicles of a Betrothed

He releases my arms and I leave them in place. He pulls me up to him and I am off of my feet. He grabs my thighs and urges me to wrap them around him. I oblige. He holds me in place. His hand leaves my thighs and slowly caresses their way to my behind. My mind is screaming for me to stop him but I am entranced by his passion. *How can this terrible soul make me feel this way?* He carries me over to the bed and lies me down. I know what comes next but I am afraid to stop him. He unravels his towel and it falls to the floor. He is totally exposed to me. His manliness is standing at attention. His body is dry now but his hair is ruffled. He looks even more delightful this way. I can see why the women of this island love this man. He climbs onto the bed and I do not move.

"Take off your brassier and underwear."

I hesitate. I sit up and I try to speak. "Sir I . . ."

"Do not speak. Just do as I ask."

I place my hands behind me and unsnap my bra. When I pull it from me I bind my breast against my body. I began to shiver. I am frightened. More than I have ever been in my life. He reaches for my hands and I release my breast. He stares at them. I turn away and look at the door.

"Do not take your eyes from me Chakori." He rubs my thigh and I inhale. Somehow his touch calms me. He reaches for my hip. He pulls at my underwear and nods at me.

I take my underwear and slide them down to my ankles. I lie back to slip them off and he grabs them.

He tosses them across the room and in an instant he straddles me.

Annetta Hobson

I feel the rock hard pole on my leg. I have never been this far with a man. My body is shaking so hard he lightly touches my shoulders to calm me.

"I am a very dangerous man. But I take my bed manner very serious. I would never hurt you this way. I enjoy gentle interactions so relax. You will learn to enjoy this. It is the best part of a marriage."

"But . . . but . . . we are not married. I really wanted to wait." I close my eyes so I will not see what is coming next. I know I must have angered him. I just wait for the monster to appear.

He huffs.

And the next thing I feel is his lips on my neck. He kisses it intensely. I roll my eyes open then closed again. He is driving me to the brink of insanity.

He grabs my waist and kisses me harder. His lips trail down to my breast and I am lost. My hips rise from the bed. He pushes them down. He spreads my legs apart and dips one finger inside. It feels much like it did when I tried it but better. I moan. I part my lips and moan again.

"Place your hands in my hair." He demands.

Unaware of my grip, I release the bed and rub my fingers through his nearly dry hair.

He leans up and closes his eyes. He moans at my touch.

"I want you so badly. Do you want me to enter you now?"

I am shocked by his question. I do not know how to respond. He realizes my dilemma and kisses my lips. He lifts his behind in the air and dips into my parted thighs. When he places his hand over his manhood to enter me there is a knock at the door.

Chronicles of a Betrothed

I pull away from his kiss. I grab my lips which are puffed from our assaulting kisses.

"Mistress Chakori may I enter?"

I am afraid. I don't know what to say.

He smiles and jumps from my bed. He hurries into the bathroom and closes the door.

I jump up, grab my robe, and run to the door. Before I open it I look in the mirror and smooth it with my hand. My skin is red from the batter of passion he unleashed on me. I look behind me before I pull the door open. I unlock it and yank at it.

Emund stands there with his hands crossed. He notices my uneasiness.

"Is everything ok?"

"Yes. I'm fine." I say as I tighten the belt of my robe.

"First lady Surina, would like to know if you need anything before they send the attendants to begin your preparation for the introduction gala."

"Um I don't think so Emund. You can go and tell her I am ready."

He nods and takes another skeptical look at me before he starts down the hall.

I smile and lean on the edge of the door before I shut it. When I turn around Daler is fully dressed in a black suit. I fold my arms and walk towards the bed. As I pass him he grabs my arm.

"I enjoyed that. I must finish what I started, soon." He kisses my cheek and walks for the door.

"What will happen to me if Monarch Khattris finds out?" I state barely whispering.

He looks at me and smiles.

This man is beautiful beyond words.

"He will not find out. By the time we are married I will have filled your belly with my child." He straightens his jacket and leaves the room.

I am without words. *I am possibly falling for this murdering heartless person. And I hate myself for it. Elliot's body is lying in a ditch somewhere and I am moving forward with those who are responsible. I am a terrible person for it and I know it.* I slowly circle the room. I pick up my undergarments and put them away. *I might as well stay nude. The people coming next will strip me anyway.* I am slowly getting used to others seeing me this way. I have changed in a matter of a couple of days and I can't help it. Daler has wheeled me in. I have laid eyes on him all of three times and he has managed to get into places I have guarded my whole life. I sit on the bed and daydream about the possibility of having the marriage I dream of. I am taken from my thoughts when the door opens and tons of people rush into my room. Jasleen is the last to enter.

"So, are you ready to be the animal on a barbeque spit?"

I shrug. Jasleen's logic befuddles me. *How can she so clearly see the evil in her lineage and Jasmine be totally oblivious?*

"I guess I am. I have no choice."

"You are right my dear you do not." Khattris states as he enters my room. "And when you meet my son tonight, please change your attitude. He is a very hard person to impress. You are very beautiful, so physically you are fine. But if I hear of your defiance you will be sorry."

I swallow hard. If I defy him by refusing to lay with him then what? Will I be sorry?

"Tonight you will smile. You will eat like a woman of Jutesh. You will not touch any man except for Daler. Understood?"

"Yes sir."

"Good. Do you have any questions?"

"Um I do . . . when should I touch him?"

He sighs. "When he is introduced he will take your hand. I will introduce you both and after that you are his. Touch him when you like. Do you have that?"

"Yes sir. I do."

"I will leave you to be prepared." He kisses my forehead. "You are family now."

He nods to everyone and leaves the room. In an instant I am bombarded with hands. They grab at my hair and my robe. I am whisked to the bathroom and bathed. My hair is washed and I can't wait for it to end. When I am back in my room things have changed. They have a station brought in and I am taken to it. I sit and there are lots of lights around a massive mirror. My hair is dried with a device that makes a lot of noise. I close my eyes and silently drift off into my thoughts while this team of strangers works diligently. I remember the first time I met Elliot and tears tickle the corners of my lids. I am a trader. I do not deserve to live. He was murdered protecting me and I am consorting with the enemy. And to make things worse I am slowly becoming enthralled by Daler. The second most atrocious human being I have ever laid eyes on. The tears escape their resting area and begin to fall down my cheek.

"Mistress are you okay?" A girl that is fixing my hair asks me.

"I am fine. Please keep working." She nods and grabs tissue to wipe my tears. When everyone is done I am propped in front of a mirror to look at myself. *I must say I have never looked better. The dress Jasmine selected fits me like a well-made glove. I can see every voluptuous curve in my body. My face is stunning.* The thought of being this beautiful whenever I please delighted me. My thoughts are suddenly left far behind as I am swept away.

Chapter 7

Emund holds my arms as I clasp my hands together. I stand outside a grand door. It is larger than life. This building sits far behind the gorgeous estate that is my new residence. It is decorated with an array of fresh flowers outside. *I can just imagine the sight inside*. It has to be better than the vision out here. I hear live music. I have only heard such a sound recorded. I have never seen a musician in person. There were probably talented musicians on Ghatlan but I had not had the pleasure. The music fades and I hear a thunderous sound. Khattris is speaking and his voice is magnified.

"I would like to thank you all for coming. Some of you have traveled from various parts of the world, undiscovered islands such as Ghatlan, RoDania, and Mochatson. I have brought you all together to witness peace between my island Jutesh the larger of the undiscovered lands, and Ghatlan. We have been at war for many years. I believe if we are at peace the United Countries have no reason to interfere. I know we have been afraid of the UC trying to force us to combine with their Continents. But we are here today to show them that this is not necessary. We can live in peace with one another. Yes, they have several resources that we can use, but we do not have to combine with them to partake in their treasures. Ghatlan and Jutesh are now united as one under a treaty. Ro Dania and Mochatson may be urged to follow. I have the President of the UC here as a witness. My son Daler Khattris will wed the daughter of Prime Minister Roshan and First Lady Marya Desai of Ghatlan. And, one day they will rule over both islands as one. Please help me welcome Mistress Chakori Desai of Ghatlan."

The doors swing open and I am ushered into the great room. The structure is astounding. There are about 1000 people in attendance and they are all looking at me. I step into the building. The sound of my silver one of a kind shoes clacking across the floor. My heart is pounding. I try to plaster a smile onto my face but it is very shaky. Some of the faces smile back. Others just stare as if I am some sort of display to be shown. I make my way to where Khattris stands. He is stationed in the center of the room on a secure and over decorated stage. When I reach him Emund places my hand in his. I turn to my left and before I look at my feet, I spot my father and mother. They look wonderful. He winks. I assume he is not allowed to touch me until Daler arrives. I lift my dress as I step into Khattris' grasp. When I reach the top of the stairs I walk to the middle of the stage and clasp my hands together. He nods and raises what I believe is a microphone to his mouth.

"Here she is." He waves his hand towards me and the room erupts into a crescendo of applause.

I bow my head and try to keep the plastic smile on my face.

"And now for the man of the hour, the person we have all been waiting for, my son the man that will one day change the undiscovered islands and make them come together in peace as one, Daler Khattris."

The applause is so loud my instinct is to cover my ears. But I reframe from the idea. I turn to the door opposite the one I entered and he enters. He has Jasmine on one side and Jasleen at his other. They are arm in arm. They slowly approach the stage. The sea of people part so they can pass. I hear the snickering of several young women in the crowd. I look over and I spot a crowd of beautiful young women waving at him. He does not acknowledge them. But I am sure he has had at least a few of them. He makes his way to me. He releases his sisters as he steps onto the stage. His father grabs his hands and embraces him. He pats his back and passes him the microphone.

"First, I would like to say thank you to my father for entrusting me with such a great task. My heart is filled with joy as I revel in the fact that he trusts me to be as great as he is one day." His deep silky voice caresses every part of me. Why do I respond to him in such a way?

"I am honored and will do the very best to support the people of the undiscovered islands. With my new bride we will bring an abundance of peace and tranquility back to our lands. Thank you!"

He hands the microphone back to his father and turns to me.

I swallow hard. His eyes burn through me. I smile but he is stoned face. I wonder what I may have done wrong. Before my mind can travel he grabs me by my shoulders. I am shocked by this gesture. He pulls me close and kisses me deeply right there in the middle of the room. I do nothing. My hands hang beside me like lifeless fish. His hands slide down my arms and he grabs my hands. I stand there like a puppet ready for my next command. He slides his fingers in between mine and raises them in the air. He releases one hand and stands beside me with the other still hitched high. The crowd claps and I am dumbfounded. He extends the free hand toward his father to speak once more. He clears his throat. "Father there is one more thing I wish to say."

Khattris nods.

He turns to me. "I know that it is a tradition in the politics of our island to wait a year to marry your betrothed. But, I am eager to mend the rift that has plagued our islands for years. I wish to marry Mistress Chakori three months from now." There is a huge unanimous gasp throughout the room.

My father's eyes grow large. I witness as three young women cover their mouths.

"Well Daler." Khattris leans in. "I didn't expect you would want to even marry her. But this is quite a surprise. Why the rush?"

Daler covers the mic and speaks. "Father don't worry. I know what I am doing."

Khattris smiles and speaks. "Okay if it is alright with the Prime Minister you two will marry Saturday the 25 of September."

I look to my father and he nods with his seal of approval. I am flabbergasted. I have to marry him sooner than I thought. There will be no room for possibility. I thought maybe if I had time he would grow tired of me and send me home. And now he wants to marry me sooner. I am afraid. His motives are a mystery.

"I ask now Prime Minister Desai of Ghatlan, Koreen Aksunti ruler of RoDania, and Monarch Diaonti Rykii of Mochatson join

Chronicles of a Betrothed

Roman Hunter, the President of the United Countries and me for a discussion of what's to come."

Chapter 5

The people Monarch Pavan Khattris called start toward the back of the building. I stand there, unaware of what I should do next. Daler leaves with the group. I step off of the stage and Emund is there to help me down. When I step from it my mother attacks me from behind. Emund jumps into guard mode and snatches her away. I quickly stop him.

"That is my mother Emund. Please allow her access to me." he releases her arm and I embrace her.

"I did not know you two would be here."

"I would not miss it for the world. Besides it has been eons since I traveled from Ghatlan. We needed this. It further proves you have made our lives much better. Thank you daughter."

She kisses my cheek and I am reminded that she once loved me enough to protect me. I will try to forget they used me to end the war.

My mother excuses herself. She wishes to taste the exotic food Jutesh provides. I am in awe with her. Everything about this island is amazing. Excluding the murdering tyrant who runs it. I walk to find someone to speak to and I am halted by the group of women that was admiring Daler.

Annetta Hobson

"Well, well, well. You are the lucky woman who gets to share Daler's bed. I must say I did not think the women of Ghatlan looked half as decent as you."

She leans in and sniffs me.

"I hear they smell too." She laughs. "I am just kidding. I am Geena Badyal. I was supposed to be Daler's wife. We were promised from birth. I have given myself to him body and soul. So please excuse the fact that I prayed for your demise when I heard you ran." She smiles a cat like grin.

"Please do not apologize to me." I say not adding anything to my gesture. She waits for a response worth combating but she does not get it.

"I know you are a virgin because his father only wants him to have a pure bride. Unfortunately, I was a bit loose." She covers her mouth and giggles. "But he didn't mind. I was very experienced. I really know what he wants. I gave it to him all of the time."

I stand there. I do not respond. I just smile. She is taunting me for no reason. There is really no point, jealousy is not something I feel. I know nothing about him so she could have been with him thousands of times and I would not care.

"Geena will you excuse me I have a ton of people to get acquainted with, it was a pleasure meeting you. I hope you get to have him again one day."

Her eyes grow wide.

I smile and nod. She steps aside and I proceed toward the door.

"And where are you going?" Jasleen calls out.

I turn and greet her.

Chronicles of a Betrothed

"You look wonderful Jasleen. I really like your dress." She glances down at her dress and looks at mine.

"Oh, but I do not hold a candle to you tonight. You are stunning. No wonder Daler laid eyes on you and want to marry you now."

"I doubt that has anything to do with it."

"Trust me, I know him better than you. He wants to sleep with you."

"Oh I know that much." I stop talking. I feel I may give away the secret visits I have been getting from the Tyrant's son.

"And, how would you know that from a five minute meeting?" she grabs my arm and pull me to a back hall. "Have you met with Daler before?"

I bite my lip and give her a guilty look.

"Why? How? Don't you know my father will have you killed if he finds out you two have met one another?"

I panic. "It wasn't me. He came to my room. I did not know who he was at first. He said he wanted to see the hag his father promised to him. I swear nothing happened. I am still a virgin."

She smiles. "How did you resist his charms? I hear from my countless friends he has seduced that he is irresistible."

"I . . . I . . . maybe he just does not want me."

"I doubt that. I witnessed that kiss. Just like everyone else in that room. Just be careful Chakori. He is the purest form of evil. Just like my father. I have witnessed some of their malicious acts, unlike Jasmine. "

"I have witnessed a few of my own. I know who your family is. I will never forget it."

"Okay? I am going back to the gala. Are you coming?"

"Give me a minute. I need some air. I will be there shortly." She waves and reenters the gala.

I walk down the winding hall to find a way out. I hear a rumbling of voices. *Oh no, not again.* I think. But my curiosity drags me right in that direction. I peek into the slightly cracked door.

"Order! Order! Now Monarch Rykii, We have been totally honest with you. You have read the treaty. There is no trickery involved. I know you want what is best for Mochatson. But we can give them so much more combined. Koreen and Roshan have agreed to let our children rule over the islands. They are pure, a better version of all of us. Why won't you allow this change for your people?"

"You are *a murderer* and *a liar*! I do not trust you! *Koreen* how can you agree with this? It is a tactic to unite with the UC under Khattris reign. He is doing this for himself." Monarch Rykii shouts.

The president of the UC stands. "I am only here as a witness. We are very good allies with the people of Jutesh. They have the finer things. Buildings, clothes, furniture, their people have trained to be judges and doctors. Their island is modernized because of their trust in our promise not to interfere but only to observe. We have also lent Ghatlan soldiers to help the war riddled island. We are also offering to help rebuild under the terms of this treaty."

"And *what I ask is* in it for you President *Roman?*"

"We only want to be aware of all of the islands. The unknown is unsettling to us. We only want to be aware."

Chronicles of a Betrothed

"*I do not believe you!!* You are a liar also. You fraternize with this *murderer* so you are a *murderer* too!" He screams.

"Calm down please. Here are the treaties. You each get a copy. Under the new treaty, we will be called the Islands of Amity. We are our own united lands. In no way will the UC govern us. We have our own courts, our own physicians. We are even in the final stages of building a multi-level hospital. My daughter Jasmine is preparing to travel to the UC to become the chief judge of our main courts. If you would like to have candidates for these positions, we will accommodate them. I and my son will handle the dealings with the UC. Your islands will just sit back and reap the rewards."

"What of our titles? Will we still remain in leadership under Daler?" Koreen asks.

"Of course. Your people are used to their own governing entity. So there will be titles but lower positions. You will consult with Daler and I regarding major politics. Other than that changes will only be cosmetic. Now will all of you sign?"

They all stand. Desai and Aksunti sign the treaty. Khattris smiles at President Hunter. He returns a sly smirk. Rykii takes his version of the treaty and folds it.

"I will sleep on this. My people need to know what is afoot. I will have an answer for you in one week." He slides the contract under his arm and storms from the room. President Hunter gives Khattris a concerned glance. He returns.

"Do not worry Khattris. Rykii will sign he is just at the age of insanity and everything is suspicious to him. I am very excited we will finally have everything we will need. How soon can we get medical help? I have several children that were born ill on my island. We need immediate help."

"May I interject father?" Daler asks. He nods.

"I will have five of our personal physicians attend your young ones. Dr. Eveleen Agroia is the best Doctor throughout the UC and she is our head Physician. She will oversee the new multilevel hospital. She will personally escort the doctors to RoDania in two days."

"Thank you so much." She shakes the hand of all of the men in the room before she exits.

My father is the last to leave. I cannot move. I need to go but I am planted hanging on to every word of those still in attendance. President Hunter is very annoyed with Monarch Rykii.

"What are you going to do about him Khattris? His defiance threatens your whole plan. And, if you cannot handle a few islands, we would be happy to step in and handle it. Your approach is respected. But we take things by force."

Khattris huffs. "I am aware of that Hunter. That is why you have not accomplished what I have. In the matter of two weeks, I have ended this war and got them to sign a treaty. If we would have continued to do things your way, there would be no souls left on the islands to rule over."

"You are correct. We would have continued to bomb them until we could create our own population. Be very glad you were smart and decided to give in from the beginning."

"I did not give in. I got something out of it for my people. My island's scenery is more beautiful than any land the UC has combined."

Chronicles of a Betrothed

"Yes thanks to me. It would still appear the way it did when I was elected 15 years ago. After our one world government was created your land slipped through because of your distance. Then we find out there are three additional islands. We could have taken Ghatlan but we allowed you to do it your way. Fix this with Rykii or the deal is off. I will send missiles over there to destroy the entire island. It will not exist."

"Hunter that is the solution to everything for you, I will have all three islands under a treaty. And Daler will be the face of leadership. Marrying Desai's daughter ensures that."

"We shall see Khattris. I don't care either way. I just want it done. Remember the UC owns you. And soon, we will own them all."

"I run my land you just pay for it. No one owns me."

"We let you think that." President Hunter states as he buttons his suit jacket. He heads straight for the door where I am spying. I quickly examine the hall. I notice a back corner that dips. I hurry in that direction. I cannot get there fast enough. I hide deep in the crevice of this corner. It has no light so I am well hidden. President Hunter passes. I peek out and Daler and his father are heading my way. They talk as they pass.

"Father, I think you are making a mistake trusting Hunter. Their laws are made to deceive. If we continue to put our faith in them they will surely dismiss us."

"My son. I am a very smart man. I will use them. They will not bomb these islands. The precious minerals we all carry are worth more than anything they have ever acquired. If they were going to destroy our lands they would have. What we have is worth more than anything they own. And only I can harvest it. I know where and what sits on every island. And now I own it all. I have everyone where I want them. I hold all of the cards. Why do you think Ghatlan is not totally destroyed? They only destroyed certain parts under my instruction."

Daler laughs. "Thank you for everything father. I will be everything you hope and more."

"I know Daler. But please respect our traditions and leave the girl untouched. It is the only thing we have left. I have modernized our lives so much. I want a few things to remain."

"What difference does it make?"

Khattris stops and turns to him. He grabs his shoulders and look into his eyes.

"Life and death. If you grow tired of her before you are married and do not want her it will ruin everything."

"Why do you think I moved the wedding up? I want her now. I have never wanting anything as much. She does something to me."

Khattris laughs. "Daler. You always want what you cannot have."

"But I have her. And, I will have her father when I please."

He stops laughing. He is very serious now. "If you take her before marriage I will have her killed. And all of this will be for nothing. Do as I ask Daler please?"

"Yes sir." He returns.

They walk past my hiding place and continue to the gala. I peek out to make sure that the hall is clear. When I am sure I hurry back to the gala. I wander in as if I was lost.

"There you are dear. I was beginning to worry. I assumed you took one look at my son and ran for the hills." First lady Surina

Chronicles of a Betrothed

sings. As I approach she grabs me into the tightest embrace. I hug her back with care.

"I was lost. This place is almost bigger than my entire island." I joke.

"I know my darling. Well, what do you think?"

I am confused. What is she referring to? I shrug my shoulders hoping she will explain.

"What do you think of my son, Daler?"

"Oh, I think we will make fine children together. He is a very handsome man. I am pleased." *Even though he and your husband have a diabolical plan to secretly trade and deceive us with the UC... where we are all in grave danger.*

"Great. I was promised to Pavan. I was afraid at first. But when I laid eyes on him. I had never met a man more distinguished. And, he was quite a sight. He still is."

I nod. "I agree. Daler is his splitting image. Just twenty years younger."

She smiles. She loves her vile creature. And his son matches the image of his atrocity. I am locked into one of the most erroneous situations ever. I stand there and listen to her go on about the wedding. I drift away into my thoughts. My wedding to a horrible man is closer than I wanted. He wants to take me against my and his father's wishes. I will die if it is discovered. I wanted a quiet life of a soldier's bride. We almost made it. If the freight ship would have come days earlier, I would have no knowledge of all of the espionage upon us. *Wait! Did Elliot contact anyone of our departure? Is that why we were discovered?* Looking back I believe we were turned in. They arrived to siege us a day before we were to leave. I drift deeper into my thoughts. I hear the chatter from the First Lady but I cannot come back. I think of Elliot standing on a beach perched with white sand. He is dressed in all white. He stands there with a portly man holding the book. I slowly approach, my bare feet sinking into the beautiful sand. With each step I draw near. He smiles and I see every one of his glorious white teeth. He reaches out to me. I release one of my hands from the perfect bouquet of flowers I grip. I extend my hand to receive his. I am almost there. I am marrying the man I love. I touch his skin and...

"Mother are you talking Chakori to death? I don't want her to know all of our faults yet."

It is way too late for that. It is possible I know more than she does. Daler has joined us as I daydreamed. He blinds me with his devilish smile.

"I finally get to talk to you Chakori. The waiting has been strenuous. I must admit my curiosity was killing me. I'd known my first betrothed my entire life. So imagine my surprise when I was informed I would be marrying someone from Ghatlan."

I manage a smile. He is pretending to have never met me. It is really humorous. I want to be afraid of him. But every time he is near I forget everything I have learned.

"Yes I as well. I was to marry also."

"I heard." He interrupted. "But that marriage was of your own arranging, correct?"

"Yes." I answer.

"We must take on the sins of our father Chakori. And, if we stray away from that path it will be deadly for us. Do you understand Mistress?"

I feel a surge of fear. I do not know if he is referring to Elliot's demise or the possibility of my own.

"I totally and completely understand sir."

He smiles that horribly wonderful smile again. "Enough with the sir. It was fun at first, now I am annoyed. Call me by my name. I demand it."

"Yes, Daler."

"Much better." He leans close to my ear and whispers. "Now when I ravish you later, remember to whisper my name."

I clear my throat and tug and the bodice that is starting to suffocate me. As I am pulling, my cleavage presses out. I try and yank the dip back over my breast and Daler stops me.

"I like it just like that."

I feel objectified. But I am turned on. It is insane how this man brings fear and arousal at the same time. I place my hand at my sides and look to the floor.

"Daler you are frightening her. Stop it now. Show her the gentleman that I raised. Darling here."

His mother pulls the fabric and my cleavage is controlled.

"Mother please. I cannot touch her. So I need to at least be able to look at her."

I blush knowing exactly what he is implying. Surina takes my hand and waves for Daler to follow her. We exit the party and stand outside in the breezy night air. She scans the area and pulls us close before she speaks.

"Son, she belongs to you, and you alone. You may touch her. But you must not take her. I was promised to your father. And, we made things interesting. Please do not repeat what I am saying, your father would be very angry. There are things you can do to occupy your mind. Your father will encourage you to take another. But I encourage you to be true to Chakori. If you take care of your responsibilities with politics and spend time with her. It will make your wedding night more special."

I smile, First lady Surina is really sweet. She knows her son. I shy away when he stares at me. I do not know if he will take her advice. I just want to make it to the wedding. If he keeps visiting my room I will be killed. I do not have the strength or the right to refuse him.

"I hear you mother. Now, I would like to get acquainted with my bride to be, if you don't mind."

"Of course. She kisses my cheek and his. Then she slowly walks away waving. When she enters the building he grabs me. He pulls me very close. His hands tickle the small of my back. I close my eyes so they do not have to meet his. I turn my head away. He takes one hand and gently brings my chin up. I open my eyes and he is staring at me.

"I must admit I have seen a lot of women in my life. I have traveled the world. I have never in all of my years lay eyes on beauty such as yours."

I try to pull my face away from his grip but he clutches my chin.

"That day I came into your room to meet you, you peeked around that corner and I was totally entranced by a glimpse of you."

I stare unable to respond. The honesty in his eyes flows through me. His words ring true. But I am reluctant to believe him.

"Will you say something to me?"

I do not know what I should say. He is two different people. When he speaks to me, he is this seductive charmer. But when he is with his father, he is a monster bread from the depths of hell.

"I do not know what I should say."

"What do you think of me?"

I am startled by his question. I cannot reveal how I really feel. I just remain silent. When I do not answer he releases me.

"I heard about the comment you made to Geena. Why did you say that?" He takes a step away from me. He plants himself in a defensive stance. My hearts starts to race. I do not know what will come next.

"I . . . I did not understand why she was speaking to me that way. I cannot be jealous of something I know nothing about."

He smiles and relaxes. "But you told her you hope she gets me again. Is that what you want me to do? Sleep with other women until we are married?"

"I do not know what to say. I assume you will do as you please, right?"

He presses his lips together. I feel I have definitely angered him this time. He reaches his hand out for mine. I take his hand and he leads me back to the party. He never answers my question. I guess Geena will get what she desires. I will be just like First lady Surina, just the wife. Geena will be Daler's Eveleen. I am sure of it now.

Chapter 8

I sit up in my bed and stretch. The gala raged well into the evening. I watched as Daler wooed the crowd. He held my hand and we mingled. Everyone loved him. He was the highlight of the night. Not one person expressed the hatred I feel when I think about the things he does in secret. The people are fooled by him. But not me, I know the things he does in the night. When someone crosses a Khattris they die. That is surely the ill fate of Monarch Rykii. He will soon experience their wrath. I swallow hard. I feel a bit queasy.

Father never let me drink alcohol. I was allowed the occasional wine but liquor was off limits. It was rare in Ghatlan to even have it. I stand and I am light headed. I run to the bathroom and grip the toilet seat. Everything from the night before now swims the sewers of Jutesh. I stand and wipe my face. I grab a towel and decide that a bath is in order. As I bathe I relive the evening's events.

Daler did not speak directly to me for the rest of the night. *I believe our talk made him upset and he no longer is intrigued by me. I cannot say I am not disappointed. I liked the way he touched me. I just do not like him. I guess?* I wash my body and relax in the warm water. I think about Khattris and how he does Eveleen. She had his child and she does not know where the child is. *Even my father had his women. But do the women of leadership follow their own laws? Do they take lovers also?* I doubt Surina Khattris has some young man awaiting her in the night. First, she loves the vile Pavan and second he would kill her if he found out.

I would not even be thinking of a lover if I was not here. This land corrupts. I hope I do not fall into this life of wealth and lies. I am here to do a service. I will do my best. I will always be afraid of President Hunter's demands. *What will he ask of me?* I am so afraid of the unknown. Life has become too complicated.

I finish washing and step out of the bath. I past the mirror and I remember when Daler was in here, bathing. I shake myself from my thoughts, go to my closet and there are some new things inside. I slide through the rack of new garments. They are lovely. I grab one of the dainty silk blouses and slide my arm in and it rolls across my arm. The feeling of the fabric is heavenly on my skin. I see an array of skirts none like the ones I owned back home. I grab one and step into it. I pull it up and fasten it around my waist. I look divine. I resemble one of the Women in the UC. The one's in high position. The gowns were gorgeous, but these clothes make me feel important somehow. I glare at my reflection for what seems like hours. I love my new look.

Suddenly there is a knock at my door.

"Come in."

Daler steps in. My eyes grow large. I am obviously very surprised by his visit.

"Good Morning Chakori. I see you like the clothes I had sent to your room this morning."

"Yes, I love them. Why the change? I thought I was supposed to only wear gowns."

"That is what my father likes. I like you this way."

"Thank you. They are very lovely."

"My pleasure." He walks over to my bed and sits. He rubs the fabric. He looks down at the coverings and back to me. "I have a surprise for you."

I turn to look at him and I do not know how to respond. This man is so unpredictable. "And may I ask what it is?"

"Yes, you may ask, but I would rather show you. Meet me in the foyer in about 20 minutes."

"Do I need anything?"

"No just be down there, and wearing that. There are new shoes in there also."

I nod. *Where are we going? Why does he want to go anywhere with me?* I finish dressing and slide on a pair of the most exquisite shoes made. Everything about this place is impeccable. I stand and walk for the door. When I swing it open Emund is standing there. "Good Morning Emund. I missed you last night."

"I was around. I am never too far away." He smiles and I walk ahead of him.

"Do you know where we are going today?"

"Yes I do."

"Where?"

"You will find out soon."

We walk down the several flights of stairs to finally reach the foyer. Daler is already there and he has several bags packed. I become anxious. My stomach is fluttering. I step down into the foyer and all of my emotions rush me at once. I look from the bags to him.

"Are we traveling?"

"I will not say anything until I am comfortably sitting. So are you ready to leave or do you want to stand here asking questions that you will only get the answers to when we get to where we are going."

I walk to the door. Emund grabs the bags that are packed and follows me. I walk outside and there is a black shiny vehicle waiting for us. Emund places the bags in the open trunk and slams it shut. I slide into the vehicle and Daler enters behind me. Emund closes the door behind him, runs around, and jumps into the driver seat.

"Where are your guards?"

"Emund is all we need. He is very capable of protecting us."

"I'm sure he is."

We drive through the streets of the island. I could never tire of the cultivating scenes. The beautiful trees that have the island feel, and the buildings reminds me that I am in modern society. It is such a different sight from Ghatlan's frayed structure. Its war ridden roads torn apart by missiles. I am delighted Ghatlan will soon get the makeover it deserves. But I hate how it has been acquired. My freedom and sacrifice of happiness is the key to it all. But I accept it.

We arrive at an airport. I have seen airplanes but never this close.

"Are we getting on one of these aircrafts?"

"Yes, relax. You have been on it before. You were just heavily sedated."

Chronicles of a Betrothed

I swallow hard. Being above land is something I am not looking forward to. We step from the vehicle. Emund grabs our bags and we walk toward the airplane. When we reach it a man dressed in all blue greets us. He assures us that this is a perfect day for flying. We climb aboard. I nestle into the plush seat of the plane. It appears to be designed for a small amount of people. Not like the ones I read about with my tutors.

"How do you like it?"

"I guess it is fine. I have never seen the inside of one before."

He smiles. "Well, it belongs to the family so it is at your disposal, with supervision of course."

"Yes, of course. I would never run sir. I value my brother's life."

His eyes grow large. "What do you mean by that?"

"Your father warned me. I apologize."

He calms. "Nothing will happen to your family. Besides after our trip you will never want to go."

"Now that you are comfortable sir, may I ask where we are headed?"

"Yes, you may. First Chakori, I would love for you to call me Daler. Sir is something that I ask you not refer to me as. You should reserve it for my father. And since you are overcome with curiosity, I will tell you. First, I have to take care of something in Mochatson. Then we will be traveling to the United Countries. Buckle up, we are preparing to take off."

I sit back and grab hold of the armrest. My heart pounds. I am overcome with worry. Daler looks over and tries to distract me.

"Would you like a drink? Reach beside you, there is a cooler. Grab the bottle and drink. It will calm you."

Annetta Hobson

I nod and follow his instructions. I drink the liquid so fast I barely have a chance to taste it. Soon my head is swirling. I am in the air several thousand feet. I allow myself to drift off and sleep.

When I open my eyes Daler is watching a huge screen. There are beautiful images playing on it.

I blink to help my eyes focus.

"It's amazing isn't it?"

"Yes. I have never had a television. Father would never allow it. The soldiers loved it and I reframed out of respect. Father allowed us to be taught of technology, but he despised it."

He folds his arms and presses his lips into a hard line. "Well, he is definitely all for it now."

"I can imagine he is."

He lightens his expression. He unstraps himself and stands. He removes his jacket. I watch his every move. He makes anything look absolutely divine. Even the towel I saw him in fit his body deliciously. He sits on the arm of my chair. He rubs his fingers through my hair and inhales.

"Chakori, why do you not like me? I know your soldier was killed because of me. But I did not pull the trigger."

I am in shock. He never seems to fail at that. *Why would he ask me these things? How do I answer?*

"I do not know exactly how to answer that. I really loved Elliot. I will never love anyone else." I drop my head and look to the floor.

He stands and places his hands into his pockets. "I promise you this. You will love me. I guarantee it. I have feelings for you right now. I don't know why and how but you have captured me. And, I do not want to be free."

Chronicles of a Betrothed

"I have not done anything to cause you to feel that way. I just want to do what I was brought here to."

He laughs. "I am so in awe with you. I will enjoy the road to get to you. And, I will get to you." He walks away. I am left watching him as he does.

The plane ride is very tiring I feel as if we will never reach our destination. We watch the screen. I look to him and he is staring blankly at it. I turn my eyes back to the screen. I am uninterested in what is playing. When time passes I look at him again and he is chewing on something. It appears to be some sort of plastic. It hangs from his lip. He swirls it around with his tongue, while holding it between his fingers. He is slouched down in the chair. I assume it is comfortable. One hand sits on the armrest. He is especially handsome this way. I see him as a normal person who ponders just like average people do. When my eyes arrive back to his face his is looking at me. His pulls the plastic from his mouth and sit up. His eyes are burning through me. I hold my breath. He can tell I am watching him with admiration. He stares at me without saying a word. We glare at each other for a while. The magnetism between us is evident. But it is no substitution for love.

Finally he stands and throws the plastic to the floor. He starts toward me. I take a breath and do not exhale. When he reaches me I stare like an animal being stalked by a hunter. He grabs my hands and pulls me from my seat. He wraps them around his neck, something he does often. He breathes into my face. The sweet smell of mint from his mouth causes my eyes to roll. When I open them he is smiling his signature smile. Causing my knees to buckle. He tilts his head and pulls my body close to his. He kisses my lips. I am lost. I fall into it and let myself go. He does have power. The power to immobilize me with just a kiss. It becomes passionate. He pulls away and starts to unbutton his shirt. I am once again mesmerized by his body. This time I reach out to touch it. He skin is smooth. The hair on his chest lays fine and feels like silk. My hands trail across his body. I am sucked in by the heat that attracts us. He grabs the top of my blouse and rips the buttons open. I hear them drop to the floor. I take the blouse off and toss it across the cabin of the plane. He looks me over and we grab each other. The passion has caused us to be aggressive. We ravage one another. He backs me up as we kiss. I open my eyes and we are leaving the cabin.

I lift from his kiss and I turn around into a bedroom. When I turn back to him he hitches his brow. I suppose he is asking permission to proceed. I pace ahead and scan the room. I turn back to him and run into his arms. He lifts me and we stumble to the bed. He lies me down and kicks off his shoes. The hunger in his eyes grows as he removes his pants. His eyes never leave mine. I am nervous. If I proceed and Khattris finds out I could die. But at this particular moment I do not care. I slither out of my skirt and remove my underwear. I really want this now. I am tired of feeling this heat only to douse it each time we meet. He climbs the bed, when he reaches me I am out of breath. I grab his hips and bring them to me. We kiss, the assault brings my joy. I want this terrible man to take me. All of my reservations have left my mind. I no longer care about anything else. He cups my breast and tastes them. He slurps them up like milk from a dish. I bury my head into the bed. His hands beseech me. I give permission.

"Touch me Daler. Touch me there."

Chronicles of a Betrothed

His eyes drag across my body then to mine, he smiles. His hair is wild and dips into his face. I take my hand and brush it away. The smile leaves him and seriousness takes its place. He crawls backwards. When he is at my belly he spreads my legs apart. He does not speak. He dips his face between my wanting thighs. I feel a cold wet pleasure there and it is the best thing I have ever experienced. He sucks my center into his mouth I scream out. He lifts his eyes to look at me. He places one finger over his lip and mouths. "Shhhh"

I cover my mouth and begin to squirm. I do not want it to be over. Please do not let it end. He slurps me up into his mouth once more. I moan through my clenched hands. I feel combustion deep in my belly. The heat is going to explode. My body lifts from the bed. I feel myself coming to an end. He stops.

"No, no please do not stop!"

He returns to my face and kisses my lips. I taste myself on him and I do not mind. He takes my hand and places it on his scepter. I am startled by the girth.

"Put me inside you." He demands. I open my legs wider and press him into my opening. The pain riddles my body. I scream out. He kisses me gently. I calm a little but the feeling of him inside me burns. He steadies himself and does not move. I grab the spread on the bed. He slowly pulls out then slowly slides in. The motion sooths me. I relax and the feeling is ambrosial. I release the covers and slip my hands into his hair. He trails kisses from my mouth to my neck. I am back to a winding spiral. His pace picks up. I grab his bottom and assists in the plunge. Finally I am at my insanities end. I feel a burst of pleasure awaiting my permission. I give in to it and I grab him close. I explode around

Annetta Hobson

his shaft. I feel myself spill onto him. I release him and grab my hair I pull at it and he assists. He holds my face and whispers. "Open your eyes Chakori. Watch me as I pour my seed into you."

Chills attack my spine, the sound of his voice commands me. I watch as he releases all of the times we met and could not touch. He shivers and his eyes roll. I am his and I want to be. His body stiffens and he forces the rest of our passion into my belly. He collapses on top of me and I massage his now damp hair.

Chapter 9

I blink to focus. I am dazed and confused. Unclear of where I am, I struggle to sit up. When I move, Daler moans.

"Oh no!" I gasp. It really happened, that wonderful exchange was a reality. I lay my head back. He lies on my bare breast fast asleep. Somehow we are covered. I look down and he is more beautiful asleep. *How could I let this happen? Khattris will find out and I will die.* Tears build in my lids. I sniffle and my body shudders. I begin to cry. Why did I give in? I am as good as dead now. Tears fall into my hair spread out behind me. I begin to wail. Daler moves, he massages my hip and lifts his head. When he notices my tears he is alarmed.

"What is wrong? Did I hurt you?"

"No." I turn my head away and sit up. I slide to the edge of the bed and cover my face. I rest my elbows on my lap and let go. My body shakes as I weep. Daler sits up and wraps his arms around his knees.

"Why are you crying Chakori?"

"I have dishonored myself. In a lust filled moment, I have sacrificed my dignity and my life. Not even Elliot was able to take that away from me."

Annetta Hobson

"I am going to be your husband. You are not disgraced. And, you do not have to worry about my father. I will handle him. I am glad Elliot did not have you. You are mine. Your mother birthed you and prepared you for me. I know this. No other man will ever have you. You are mine and I am yours forever."

I wipe my face. I feel the bed move. He glides across the bed and sits beside me. He rubs my back gently. I lean on his shoulder and he takes me into his arms.

"No one will ever hurt you. I will be your protector from today, until we both die."

I cannot believe my ears. How is it possible for a man with such malice in his heart to actually care for someone?

"How do you feel about me now? I know this was life changing for you."

I laugh. He is just so arrogant.

"I loved it. And yes, it was life changing."

He wipes away a tear that escapes when I smile. He kisses my cheek.

"Get dressed. Emund is probably ready to burst through the door."

"Oh no! Emund. Will he tell?"

"No love, he will not." His words surprise me. *Love, he called me love. Elliot called me that because he loved me. What is Daler's reason?* I shake off my thoughts and hurry to dress.

"Will we be allowed to shower when we arrive in Mochatson?"

"I doubt it. But you can bathe when we return to the plane. This is a short visit."

"Oh okay." I remember their meeting. I hope Monarch Rykii changes his mind. Khattris may follow us here and finish the job if he still refuses. Daler opens the door. And like he suspected, Emund is standing there very upset.

"Sir, are you alright?"

"I'm fine Emund. Chakori is fine also. Relax." He pats his back as he passes.

Emund eyes me as I slide by him.

"I will continue the flight inside the pit. Please fasten yourselves in we are landing."

I quickly sit and fasten myself in. I glance over at Daler and he is in deep thought. He picks up a portfolio and opens it. He begins to go over some papers. He does not look at me. I watch him for a long time and he does not even acknowledge my presence. *I knew it was too good to be. He loves no one. He is a heartless, a Tyrant in training. I feel like an idiot because now I am falling for him.*

The plane begins to descend. I brace myself for the landing. As I grip my armrest I turn to Daler. His eyes are closed. He doesn't even want to look at my face. When the plane lands, Daler places on his jacket and a tie. I am enchanted by his presence. *Now that he has had me, I am under a spell.* He walks over to me.

"I am so sorry for ruining your shirt earlier. I will purchase another when we get to the UC. That was where it is from."

"No, I am fine. I do not care about that."

He takes the back of his hand and caresses my jawline. I shiver at his touch. I long to be beneath him again.

He takes my hand and we exit the plane. I lean into his touch and grab his arm with both hands. I cling to him like my life depends on it. I smile as we walk. A small group of guards meet us at the end of the path. Their island has no port for planes. They bow and we follow them. I spot Monarch Rykii's home. It is dilapidated as some of our buildings on Ghatlan. We walk for what seems to be miles. I stop and remove my shoes. Emund quickly grabs them from me. We finally reach the doors. A young woman opens them and greets us.

"Welcome to our island. We are surprised by your visit but we welcome you." She begins to walk.

"Follow me. I am Ciria Rykii Daughter of Monarch Rykii." She looks back at me. She watches how I cling to Daler.

"You are very lucky... If I were promised to you sir I would have been most happy. Maybe I may visit your land and get acquainted also?"

Fire surges through me as she speaks. She dares flirt with him in my presence. I am enraged. I want to attack her. I lift my head from Daler's arm and release him a little. My eyes burn the back of her silky hair that flows down her back, much like mine. Her skin is like mine also. The people of this island favor my people a lot. She sways as she walks. She periodically looks back to smile at my husband to be. Daler notices my anger. He smiles and touch my face. When she notices the exchange she stops.

"You can turn up here to your right my father is in his office." Daler releases my arm and urges me forward. Emund takes hold of me and leads me on. I do not take my eyes from them as we walk.

"May I visit your land soon?" her catty voice chimes.

"You may visit whenever you like."

Chronicles of a Betrothed

"Can I leave with you? I hate it here. I have heard ramblings about your modernized island. That is where I want to be."

He smiles my beautiful smile at her. "I will call my father. You would be out of here by morning." She claps and kisses his cheek.

I stop in my tracks. Emund tries to push me on but I will not move. I stomp back to where they are standing.

"Daler my love, let's go." I say. He looks at me and smirks. I look to her and say.

"Your father should have signed the treaty. Do not try and woo what belongs to me, so you may have the finer things. Tread carefully my dear, I am territorial." I grab Daler's arm and we proceed to the office of Monarch Rykii. I look back at her with the foulest grimace and she is terrified.

Emund smiles and walks beside us.

When we reach Rykii's office the door is partially ajar. Emund pushes it open and we step in. Monarch Rykii sits in a large ancient tribal chair. It reminds me of the chairs our ancestors set in. He stands and I survey the room. There is one guard, a very large one.

"What an unpleasant surprise. Did your father send you to get my refusal in person? I am surprised he did not send an assassin to finish me off."

"My father is unaware of my visit. I came here with my bride to be to try and talk some sense into you, but it seems your mind is made up. Are you refusing to sign the treaty? And, is it your final word."

"Not only do I refuse. I spit on your treaty!" He gathers up a mouthful and spits at us.

Annetta Hobson

I jump back just in time. It hits the floor in front of us. I am disgusted. I frown and turn away. Emund pulls me away from Daler. He looks at the gesture that landed in front of us on the floor.

"Now do you not think that was a bit disrespectful?"

"Disrespect runs in their family!" I say before I can stop myself.

Emund pulls me back, and covers my mouth with my hand.

"I am sick of your father trying to bully me. I have been harassed by your family for ten years. I am tired. Now leave! Get out of my home and off my island now! Maybe when Ciria inherits this land you can persuade her. But as for now, you can go! Leave this instant!"

Daler approaches him. The elder man is unafraid. This is a very strong minded gentleman. And he has no one but Ciria, his bride died years ago from a disease that plagued his island.

He watches Daler carefully as he approaches. His guard readies for what may come.

Emund releases me to follow him.

Daler pulls a contract from his coat jacket and hands it to him. "Do not be a fool, sign the treaty." The man snatches it and rips it to shreds. When he is done he smacks it in Daler's face.

He closes his eyes and turns to Emund. He nods and then bends down. He reaches into an ankle strap and pulls out a hunting knife. Quickly, Emund grabs his gun from the holster and shoots the guard.

I cover my mouth. The shot is not heard. He has a black extended tip on it that muffled the sound. I look behind me and no one comes in to save them.

Chronicles of a Betrothed

Daler steps forward grabs Rykii and says. "It is your daughter's time to rule!" he plunges the knife deep into his chest and twists it, just like he did with Eveleen's brother.

I gasp. I do not let my scream out. He just killed a man right in front of me. He wipes the knife off on the dead man's robe and hurries over to grab me. At first I do not move but Emund grabs me from the other side and they drag me down the hall. I kick off my shoes once more and when we get outside of the house we run. The guards look puzzled and scurry to get inside. We run so fast my heart is pounding. *They are going to kill us. We will die today*. Before I know it I see the plane.

"Start the plane!" Emund yells.

The pilot hears him and starts the engine.

We make it to the plane and board. I am out of breath. We fasten ourselves in and the plane takes off.

Emund looks out of the window and the plane ascends into the air. When we are safely in the clouds Emund unsnaps himself and retires to the cockpit.

Daler is out of breath. I stare at him. I cannot believe what has happened. I unfasten my belt. I stand to leave the main cabin and walk through the bedroom to the bathroom. I start a bath and begin to undress. *I feel dirty. I have had intercourse today and to top I witnessed a murder. This time he knew I was present. I am promised to a mad man that I have to marry. He has had all of me.* I step into the hot water and sink into the small bath. I lay my head back and close my eyes. Silence surrounds me. I take a washcloth and lay it over my face. When I remove it and open my eyes Daler is sitting beside the bathtub on the floor.

"I suppose you are afraid of me now?"

Annetta Hobson

I sigh. "I have been afraid of you before I even lay eyes on you, when I was still safe on my island. I know who you are Daler. You are being the man I know you are."

"Does that change how you feel?"

"How do I feel? I do not know."

"You care for me. I saw it in your face when Ciria was flirting with me."

I blush because he knows. I wipe the water from my face, and shake my head. "I am in too deep. There is nothing that I can do. I have given myself to you and now I am trapped."

He drops his head. "I do not want you to feel trapped. That is why I don't want anyone else. I want you to love me, not fear me. Everyone fears us. The women allow me to do what I please when they are with me because of fear. You did not give in because of fear. It was desire."

"Daler, I believe women fear you. But they give themselves to you because you are handsome and desirable. How could you not know that? I almost gave myself to you in the room that day because I was afraid I would die if I refused."

He stands. "I told you before, no one is going to do anything to you. And, I know for a fact, you did not give in because of fear. I felt the way your body answered to my call. It responded to my every touch."

"Did you not feel me shivering beneath you? I was terrified."

He takes his hand and wipes his mouth. He smiles and massages his beard. "You were shivering only from fear?"

I smile shyly. "I must admit, you do know the way around a woman's body. Not that I am an expert in the matter." I stand and the water splashes from me. I grab a towel that is lying on the sink. I wrap it around my body. Daler hungrily watches my every move. I step onto the floor and he grabs me from behind. I stiffen at his touch. He leans close to my ear and whispers.

"May I have a repeat performance from earlier?"

I close my eyes. The heat from his breath surges through my ear and deep into my belly. I spin around to face him. I immediately kiss him, forgetting completely about the atrocious acts committed. I push him against the wall and we attack one another. He snatches my towel away from me and I am exposed once again for his every pleasure. He takes my shoulder and pushes me away.

"I want you to do something for me."

"What?" I say breathless. He unzips his pants and removes his rock hard desire for me to see.

He rubs it and place my hand on it. "Massage it like this." He guides my hand. I stroke it. It begins to tighten. The skin on it feels like smooth warm leather. I move my hand up and down. He closes his eyes and leans into the wall.

"Put your mouth on it Chakori." He whispers. I stop rubbing. I am totally confused. He opens his eyes and looks down to it then back me. He places his hands on each side of my head and pulls it toward his waist. I lower to my knees and place my lips around it.

"Wet your lips and slide them onto it gently. Do not let you teeth touch my skin." I lick my lips and ease them down, slipping it into my mouth with care. I do not know what I am doing but he rubs my head and moans.

"Oh my sweet Chakori, that feels terrific. Move your head up and down. Don't let it slip out."

Annetta Hobson

I follow his every instruction. I place my hands on his bottom to bring him in. I close my lips around him and slurp. I bob my head back and forth hoping I am doing it correctly. Suddenly, he grabs my hair and thrusts his behind forward. He pulls me up and turns me around. I am now facing the door. He gently enters me from behind. I let out a moan, it feels so delightful when it slides in this time. The sensation commands my insides. I am immediately propelled to ecstasy. He rocks back and forth. It is like he is dancing. But this dance is just for us, only for this moment. I scream and the feeling of release consumes me. Soon he lets out a groan and we slide to the floor. He pulls me onto his lap and I lie back resting my head on his shoulder.

He runs his fingers through my wet hair and we sit there reveling in our afterglow. I start to think. My heart is softening for this man. I think I could actually love him one day. But how?

"Why did you do that in front of me, Daler?"

His hands come to a halt. He takes a deep breath. "I will not hide who I am from you. You will be my wife so you must know me inside and out. You say you already do so why are you asking?"

"It's just some things I would not want you to know I am aware of. It puts me at risk."

"Your words are empty. I am who I am deal with it." he pushes me forward and stands. He yanks his pants up and fastens them. He storms from the bathroom and slams the door shut.

I am left naked and wallowing in my stupidity.

Chapter 10

I walk into the bedroom of the plane. I find something to wear inside the luggage that was packed for me. *He really has grand taste.* I should be still frightened from seeing several men killed in the last week. And for some reason, I am becoming numb to it all. I still fear the deeds of the Khattris men. I leave the bedroom and enter the cabin. I sit in my seat and prepare a drink. I sip the liquid from my glass. It tastes wonderfully. I do not look at him. He is looking through his papers again. I hear a ringing and Daler speaks.

"Hello father. I know I was supposed to wait but Rykii disrespected me . . ."

"I know father. But . . ."

"No matter how you look at it our problem is solved. And, his daughter desires a life like ours. She will have no problem signing. Go over there in the morning. Take several guards. They have very little protection. I assure you we have them. It is over . . "

"I will inform President Hunter. Don't worry we have everything we need now."

Annetta Hobson

"I will be gone for about two weeks. My bride to be needs to be educated in modern things."

"I have not touched her father! Stop worrying about me. Everything is in order. Goodbye."

He still does not look at me. I continue drinking and my eyes start to close. I stand and go back to the bedroom. I spot Emund walking from the restroom and I ask.

"How long before we reach the UC?"

"One day."

"Thank you."

I change into a night gown I find in my bag and slide under the sheets. I lie there staring into the night as I drift into a slumber.

I open my eyes. The sunlight bounces through the airplane, pinging off of the metals objects in the room. I look around. It is obvious that Daler decided against joining me. *I am not surprised, after I ruined our moment with that questioning conversation. Maybe I should have waited until after we were dressed and not naked soaked in our passion.* But I do not feel as bad. *He is the murderer right? Of course. I do not need a time or place to address the fact that he murdered a man right before my eyes.* I lay there, no use of getting up. We will not be in the United Countries until early tomorrow morning. I would rather not stare at Daler. Especially when he is agitated. After my interrogation his father completely chewed him out. I turn over and close my eyes once more. I sleep off and on all day.

Emund peeks in.

"Mistress, would you like anything to eat? You have not left the room all day. I know you must want something."

"No, I am fine Emund. I am just tired. I will sleep the rest of the trip. Please close the door behind you."

"Yes. If you change your mind there is an intercom next to you. Call and I will come." He turns to leave. "Are you feeling ill?"

"No, I am just really exhausted. I have been through so much the past couple of weeks."

He steps into the room and close the door. He walks over and sits on the bed. I do not sit up to greet him. "Mistress, let me inform you of something." He turns to look at me.

I press my fist into the bed and sit up. The tone in Emund's voice lets me know he is getting ready to reveal something.

"I have been guarding this family for many years. So I have witnessed many things." He pauses. "I have also performed a long list of revolting deeds for them. I am sorry you were forced into this life. But in order to survive you must not let it consume you. Forget what you have seen. Put it away deep into the depths of your mind. If you do not you will not survive. And, I really want you to survive. Please, if you never listen to me again heed this warning. If they think you are a threat they will eliminate you. Okay?"

I nod. Everything he says rings true.

He stands and walks to the door before he exits he says. "I will bring you something to eat now."

I slide to the edge of the bed and let my feet dangle. I stare at them and reflect on Emund's words. *When he returns with the food I eat it all.* I guess I was hungry after all. I set the dish aside and lie back down. This time I sleep until the plane is about to land. I begin feeling a bit refreshed. Daler enters the room.

Annetta Hobson

"The plane is about to land. You need to get dressed and buckle yourself in. You have about 15 minutes."

He leaves as quickly as he entered. I dress and join him in the cabin. I sit into the seat and fasten myself in. the planes descends. I look over and out of my window. The sight is extraordinary. It is Jutesh magnified; there are so many buildings and people. I am taken by such an image. As the plane draws close to land we circle over an airport. It looks much like the one in Jutesh but it is ten times the size. My eyes light up like a child. I am so impressed.

The plane lands. I am too anxious to get out and explore this place. I rip myself from the seat and hurry toward the door. Emund grabs our bags. When we exit and there is the most luxurious vehicle awaiting. The man steps out and greet us. We get into the car and we begin a scenic travel. I keep my eyes glued to the window. I stare at the various buildings we past.

"Where are we? What part of the United Countries are we in?"

"We are in the main states, where the President resides. This state is called Shashburg. After you are settled in the President wants to meet with you. How long will you be visiting us?"

"Two weeks. Unless I change my mind." Daler blurts.

I turn to look at him and his lips are firmly pressed into a line. *I don't understand his anger. He killed someone in front of me. And now his is angry I spoke of it. What kind of logic is that?*

We arrive at the hotel. We get out of the car. There is so much technology here. Everything is run by computers. Emund grabs my arm and Daler walks ahead. We follow behind. Daler steps up to the counter and speaks. The lady asks him to speak into the screen propped on the counter.

Chronicles of a Betrothed

"I am Daler Khattris of Jutesh. I have a reservation for two penthouse suites."

"What. Is. Your. Method. Of. Payment. Mr. Khattris?" the computer asks.

He pulls a card from his pocket and the screen scans it.

"Thank. You. Sir. Have. A. Nice. Stay."

The lady hands him two plastic cards.

"Here are your keys, sir. The gentleman to your left will take you to your rooms."

The man nods and we follow him to what I know as elevators.

I am so glad my tutor taught me about some of the things in modern society. I step onto the elevator and I am afraid. The doors close and I take a deep breath. The ride is smooth to the top. It comes to a stop and the doors open. The penthouse is straight ahead. It is such a wondrous sight. I walk forward with my mouth open. I love the UC. All of the luxuries are more than I could imagine. *And to think I would have experienced it all with Elliot.*

Emund smiles. He is delighted in my child like admiration. I hurry through the halls of the penthouse. I am so excited. I am actually here in the United Countries after all of the turmoil. I am in Shashburg where Elliot was deployed from. *Oh! Maybe I can meet his family.* I stop in my tracks. I turn and look down the empty hall. Daler will never allow this. I am here with my Tyrant husband to be. I must remember that from now on.

I walk into a room. I stand there and think. *I am ready for any adventure that this land may bring.* I walk to the window and stare out of it. I lean on the window pane and watch as vehicles race by. They look like a colony of bugs from this view. It makes me happy because I am finally thinking about something other than the events of the past weeks. I stand there for so long. No one even bothers to disturb me. I wonder where they are. When I search the room I am alone.

The past few weeks in Shashburg have been mind-boggling. I have learned so many things from the women here. Daler has made sure they do not teach me too much of the wrong things. They are not subject to their husbands here. Marriage is equal. No mate has authority over the other unless it is established. I have spent the majority of my time with Emund. But the experience is a one I surely want to experience again, often. Daler has steered clear of me. I have no idea why but I have not let it absorb my thoughts. From the first day of our arrival he has been occupied. I suspect he has had to deal with the backlash of Rykii's death. But I can predict Ciria is living comfortable by now. I will have to worry about her when we return to Jutesh.

I long for Daler to come into my room and take me some nights but he sleeps in another suite. Emund shares mine. *When we entered the hotel I thought we would be staying together. But I was mistaken. I am sad that he is so distant from me after our passion among the skies. I miss the way he watched me. Maybe he has tired of me. Or maybe he realized the intrigue was heightened by my pureness and now that he has taken me, I am no longer a mystery.*

I was invited to dinner at the President's Manor. He and his family will be present. I went to a few of their garment shops here. They call them boutiques. I purchased an exceptional gown. It has stones that adorn it. They twinkle when the light hits it. *I love this gown. I have nothing like it. Not even on the island of Jutesh.*

Chronicles of a Betrothed

I paired the most exquisite shoes with it. I am very anxious to wear it. I really could have imagined a life here. I would not have been this wealthy but I like it here. I bathe and sit at the well-crafted station to style my hair. I pull my hair to the top of my head and firmly secure it there. It is very appealing. I place on some extravagant jeweled earrings with a bulky necklace that matches the gown. I run to the room and dress. I look in the mirror and I resemble the women in books. I do not resemble my former self.

When I am ready I wait by the elevators for my escort. They open and Emund step from them. He looks very nice in a black tuxedo. I smile as he holds his arm out for me. I grab a hold and we step in and descend to the main floor. I appear as royalty. The kind from the tales I have heard. We are taken from the hotel to the President's home. Daler is still not present. We enter and we are directed to the main dining hall. I hear soothing music being played by musicians as we approach. Several people are in attendance. I smile as I enter. They stand to greet me. Everything about this place is grand. No wonder Khattris trades with them. I am envious that my father did not think of it first.

"Welcome to the United Countries, Mistress Chakori Desai of Jutesh by way of Ghatlan."

"Thank you President Hunter. It is a pleasure to be here. You continents are enchanting. There is none that can hold a candle to them."

"Not even the lovely undiscovered islands?"

"Not even Sir." He greets me with a kiss to my freshly painted hands.

"I see that you are enjoying what the UC has to offer."

Annetta Hobson

"Yes, I love this. I must hire someone to come home with me. Even my feet have been painted."

He laughs. "My wife does it quite often. Here she is." He extends his hand to a lovely dark skinned woman. She is tall and beautifully curved. Her eyes are deep and they entrance you. "This is Melody Hunter, my wife, the First Lady of the United Countries."

She shakes my hand. "It is such an honor to meet you Mistress Desai."

"Please call me Chakori, First Lady Hunter."

"Only if you call me Melody. Come and have a seat in the lounge room. Dinner will not be served for another hour or so."

We walk down the historical halls of the Presidential Manor. I look at the paintings of the men who ruled these continents before. I am impressed with their government. It is nothing like ours.

We enter the Lounge room and Daler is there, waiting. There are other men of importance present. I am surprised when he stands, takes my hand and gently brushes his lips across it.

"Good evening. You look marvelous."

"Thank you, I return shyly."

"Please come and sit, we were discussing our islands history."

"Enlighten me."

He ushers me to a lavish plush couch and we sit. A man that has long gray hair with a gray beard to match starts to speak.

"As I was saying, four hundred men took their families and fled the UC. They did not agree with the combining of all of the governments. They felt great danger would follow. I hear they traveled until they were so far away. They thought they would die before finding land. But they came across an island. Which I believe is known as Mochatson. It was the first to be inhabited. The men agreed they needed one man to govern them. They had knowledge of the UC's ways of life so there was doubt they would survive. When he became drunk with power, half of the fleet recognized it and tried to return. But they found Ghatlan. They said they would not choose a leader because it corrupted the men of Mochatson. They lived in perfect harmony. Soon Jutesh and RoDania was discovered and in habited.

"That was several hundred years ago. The people of your islands never knew their origin was the same as ours. Just from different continents. We are all brothers Daler. We were just returned to one another two decades ago. And now we are reuniting.

"Do a fine job young Khattris. I know your father and you are different then him. You will connect us all I am sure of it."

I am speechless. If the words this man speaks are true. We have inherited a lie. And only Khattris knew. I say nothing. I nod and smile.

Chapter 11

When dinner is ready we are summoned to the dining area. The rest of the guests are seated when we arrive. I walk to my seat and Daler helps me sit. I watch as he sits beside me smiling. His hand very carefully grazes my chin. I stare blankly not understanding the sudden affection. All of our time here has been spent at a distance. The room is noisy with separate discussions. The chattering misses me. I have nothing to say to anyone. I am a stranger here. My eyes search the room for Emund. I spot him at another table eating. I wonder if the gentlemen that accompany him are guards also. My heart is pounding I do not want to be here anymore. Daler turns to me. He notices my anxiousness.

"What is it?"

"I do not know. Maybe I just need to sleep. I have been burning the midnight oil all week." I lean in and whisper.

"No you cannot leave yet. These people must see us united. They are investing a lot of faith in this agreement. Our marriage is the key to the treaty and they are making sure we do not detour from our tasks."

I frown. I knew the affection he bestowed upon me was rehearsed. He is putting on a theatrical performance and the United Counties government are the audience.

"Do not worry. I would not ruin this. I am being the perfect supporting performer. I am aware of the consequences." I whisper. So only he can hear me

Annetta Hobson

He wipes his mouth with a napkin, places it on the table and grabs my arm. I immediately stand so no one notices his irritation with me. I smile as I rise.

"Please excuse us." I mouth as we exit the grand Dining room. I have to shuffle to keep up as Daler drags me along. He is fuming with anger. Fear attacks me. *What if he decides I am no longer valuable? Marriage to Ciria would fulfill the treaty just the same.* My strength leaves me. Confidence no longer fills me. I am suddenly afraid of where he is leading me. I take a deep breath and gulp. I stumble along beside him as he storms through the corridors. We turn and turn. I wonder where we will end up. He pulls me down a flight of stairs. I tumble down each one by one.

Oh no. He is taking me to a secluded area. He will kill me I am sure of it. When we reach the basement he turns knobs, searching for an open door. I look behind me hoping Emund decided to follow. But there is no sign of him. He would never defy Daler. I am wishfully thinking. Finally a knob turns. He pushes the door open and step in. He looks around and it is a utility room. It is the largest one I have ever seen. He slams the door and releases my arm. I back deep into the corner. I clutch my chest. My breathing is ragged. Tears build in my eyes. My made up face starts to melt. I wipe the tears as he approaches. When he gets close to me, I shut my eyes. I press them close so hard that the tears spill down my cheeks. I wipe them away and my hands are stained with colors that enhanced my beauty. The closer he gets the further I delve into the corner. I let out a wail.

"Please do not kill me Daler!" I say as I shield my face from a potential blow. But I do not feel the throttle of death. I do not open my eyes for a moment. I listen to hear if he is still near.

He sighs. "What is wrong with you? How many times do I have to tell you I am not going to hurt you Chakori?" He pauses to catch his breath. "But you will not speak to me in ill-mannered tones. Do you understand me?"

I release my face from my make shift shield. I straighten my hair and wipe my eyes.

"I'm very sorry Daler." I sniff. "I am just frustrated with you. You have ignored me since our moment on the plane. I thought you no longer desired me, and since I spoke out of the way to you. I feared my life would end."

He laughs. "What will I do with you? Must I come out and say it?"

"Say what?" I say as I find something to clean my face.

"You have to hear this in order to get over the insane fact you are going to die at my hand."

"Hear what? I am utterly confused. I don't know what you are trying to say. I'm afraid you will have to spell it out Daler."

He wipes his mouth. His fingers linger at his beard. He massages it and then scratches at it. He is stalling and I am anxious to find out why. He looks to the door and then to me.

I shuffle around the room trying to fix the mess that I have made of my face. I find a wash towel and wet it in the basin. I begin to wash my face. I rub until it is clear.

"I am in love with you Chakori, hopelessly and relentlessly in love. And I have never felt this way about another soul on this planet. My feelings for you now occupy the space in my heart that was once filled with emptiness and malice. Please believe me when I say I have been genuinely taking care of our governmental affairs. I would not stay away from you intentionally. Yes I was angry on the plane, but only because you know what I am capable of. You have witnessed it. I fear you could never love me in return."

He stares desperately into my eyes. His expression is that of a lost child, helpless and without hope. I am baffled by his admission. I search deep into the depths of my heart to find an answer. I gaze at him for a moment. He is especially handsome tonight. The suit he is wearing fits him perfectly. He is trimmed and his hair is a neat mess. Just the way I like it. His expression saddens me. The sight of him in shambles pains me.

"How do you know you love me? You have never experienced it before. You may not know what it is."

"Well . . . how did it feel with your soldier?"

I do not want to do this. But I will oblige him. I fold my arms and begin to pace back and forth. "Alright." I take a deep and exaggerated breath before I speak again. "I knew I loved him when the thought of him leaving made me ill. I would lie in my bed and daydream about being his wife. I imagined a life of laughter and lots of children . . ." I smile at the thought but instead of imagining Elliot's children I am imagining Daler's. I see a young boy with his deep blue eyes and coal black wavy hair. I see a beautiful baby girl with my brown eyes and no hair. I see my belly swollen and I am laughing, happy that I am living life with him. My eyes grow wide. I love him. I cannot believe what I am saying. How do you fall in love with a man like him?

"I know. I love you Chakori and I cannot wait until you are officially mine."

Chronicles of a Betrothed

I clasp my hands together and begin to rock back and forward. My epiphany along with his admission has rendered me speechless.

He steps close to me again. I recoil.

"What? I told you I would never hurt you."

"I'm so sorry I . . . I fear that I may also love you. As afraid as I am of you. I think about you all of the time. I can really imagine us together and I am happy with that."

He smiles my illuminating smile.

I shyly look away.

"So what about my deeds?"

"I will stay out of political affairs. How is that?"

"That sounds like you really love me."

"I am afraid I do."

He grabs me and kisses my lips. I lose myself in his familiar embrace. I wrap my arms around his waist and I am where I have longed to be. For the past few weeks this is what I have missed, nothing else. I push him against the wall and a shelf of translucent bottles spill onto the floor splattering. I jump and we laugh.

"How about I meet you in your room later? We will end this evening with something we both desire. He leans in and softly touch his lips to mine.

I close my eyes and revel in it.

"Emund is probably searching for us. We need to return. But I will see you later this evening. Do not be afraid. Know you are my life now." He whispers with our lips still glued together. He grabs a hold to my hand and we return to the dinner. When we reach the door, he stops me. I quickly look to him in confusion.

Annetta Hobson

"I wanted to give you something earlier. But you spoke rudely to me which angered me. But after my admission I really want to do this. He places a box in my hand and I look at it. He pops it open and takes a ring out of it and slides it on my finger. I am speechless.

"Here in the UC the men ask the woman they love to be their wife, after months or years of dating. They say our traditions are ancient. I believe in our methods because we always come out as the victors. But I think this will prove my feelings for you further. I have witnessed local women beam after this. So . . ."

He smiles as he slides the ring onto my finger. It is the biggest most dazzling diamond. I am very happy.

"I love you Chakori. Wear this ring so that everyone will know." He holds my hand as we reenter the dining area. We take our seats at the table and I notice Emund has left. He is likely searching the grounds relentlessly for the two of us.

After an unbelievable evening I leave happier than I could ever imagine.

Emund accompanies me on the ride home. I am so happy. I smile for the duration of the trip home. Emund periodically watches me. He eventually smiles with me from the giddiness that fills the vehicle. I stare at the gorgeous stone that sparkles in the spurts of moonlight.

"Are you feeling better mistress?" Emund asks as his smile fades.

"Oh yes Emund, I am wonderful."

"I'm very happy to hear that."

I glare at my new ring and I do not know why I am so mesmerized by it. Maybe because it is from the man that I am

Chronicles of a Betrothed

absolutely and completely in love with. I look up from this jewel that has me hypnotized, and glare out of the window. I reminisce about when he last touched me. I am overjoyed by the thought. We arrive in front of the hotel. I know that it is very late.

Emund steps out and escorts me to our room.

I go into my suite and start to undress. As the dress partially rolls from my body I imagine that it is Daler undressing me. I brush against my bare breast and it sends a chill through me. I close my eyes and I am on the plane thousands of feet in the air. Daler is entering me and it feels so nice. I never knew such a frowned upon act would feel so divine. I step out of my gown still clutching my left breast. The nipple hardens. My sinful thoughts have taken over my senses. I stand in the middle of my room in just my underwear and a pair of high heeled shoes. I rub around and explore the tingle I feel as my nipples swell and harden. I close my eyes and imagine that I am cradled in his arms. I let out a slow and sensual moan. My lips part and I drag my hand across my belly to my center. I look behind me and my door is closed. The feeling is too enslaving to stop. I want to feel end. I have to release now. I slide my underwear down my legs. With them resting on the tip of my heeled shoe I kick them across the room. I lie on the bed and spread my legs apart. I caress the bulb. The feeling sends me to another world. I dig my head into the fabric, my hair unravels. When I turn I feel the pins. I snatch it loose. I lift my head and shake it free. I lie back and dig my heels into the mattress to continue my exploration.

"Why did it take me to travel to different lands to experience this pleasure? First Jutesh now here. The years of built up frustration could have been satisfied." I say out of breath. I take my hand and massage my breast. The sensitivity drives me insane. I leave that hand in place and slide my right hand down to my pleasure center once more. I rub and caress simultaneously. I close my eyes tight longing for the burst of gratification that is unleashed at the conclusion of this endeavor. I moan. I get closer and louder with each methodic stroke of my hand. My chest rises and falls. My breathing is heavy.

Suddenly I feel a wet tingling sensation on my ankle. I open my eyes and Daler is crouched at the edge of the bed. Watching like a jungle cat ready to strike. He lifts from kissing my leg. I remove my hand and cuff my chest with my arms. I am beyond embarrassed. He lifts each foot. One after the other and he removes my heels.

"What did I tell you about starting things without me?" He says as he drops my foot and rounds the bed.

I attempt to sit up and he raises his hand. "Stay down. I am really enjoying this, my love."

I do not know whether I should smile or what. So I do nothing. He drags his hands along my leg as he approaches. His eyes are dark and he is obviously bothered by my expedition.

"I'm sorry that I interrupted you. But I must join in." he loosens his tie and snitches it off. He takes off his jacket. And before I know it he is completely naked. His clothes lay in a pile in the middle of my room floor. I watch him still clinching my breast.

"The first day when I entered your room in Jutesh I heard your moans. I wanted to rush into the bathroom and take you right then. But I did not want to alarm you. So to finally see what I missed. Ummm . . ." he moans.

Chronicles of a Betrothed

"Go ahead my darling touch yourself." He demands.

I close my eyes and release my breast. I take one hand and place it between my thighs and begin again. Soon I am lost in ecstasy. When I open my eyes again he is hovering above me, watching with wanting eyes. He places his hand over mine and starts to control it. I am his puppet and he is the master. I moan and moan. When I am at the edge he stops. He leans over and kisses my lips. I release my center and wrap my arms around him. He opens my legs further and climbs between them. Our kiss deepens and he enters me. My moisture sucks him in. I let out a sigh of relief. Finally I am back where I have dreamed of being, beneath his glorious touch, him buried in my longing. My hips answer his bodies call. Our bodies' rock to the rhythm of a song played in our minds. The pace picks up and he is thrusting into me. I hold him close. I feel myself at the brink of release. He slides out and then with one glorious thrust I spiral into a sea of emotions. My body shudders and I cannot stop. I shake until every ounce of my end is around him. He buries his hands in my hair and grabs hold. He presses my head into the bed as he follows me into paradise.

He drops on his back beside me, breathless. He places his hand over his eyes and lets out a long sigh.

"I have missed the inside of you Chakori."

I sit up and slide underneath the covers. I am so glad he joined me. I turn away so he cannot see the grin spread across my face. I feel the graze of his hand across my back. He massages it and I feel him turn to me. He kisses the back of my head. He wraps me into his warm embrace and we fall asleep.

Chapter 12

When I wake we are intertwined. My heart beats as I watch him sleep. I stare as he breathes into my face. I do not know how we ended up face to face, but I am glad. He appears as innocent as a babe. I plant soft kisses on his face. I'm careful not to wake him. I slide from his grip. I slip into my robe and leave the bedroom. In the living area of the penthouse I go over to the table and pick up the phone. I dial and order us a meal. I hang up and when I turn Emund is standing there.

"Good morning Mistress. Did you sleep well?"

"Y. . . yes." I answer completely surprised.

"Do not worry about me mistress. I am loyal. I will not disclose anything you do not want me to."

I touch my lips remembering my night. I smile and look to Emund.

"Thank you. I love him, and we will be married so there is no need to . . ."

He interrupts me. "You are correct, there is no need."

Annetta Hobson

Soon I hear a tapping on the door. I tighten the belt on my robe and hurry to open it. I grab the tray from the man and nod. Emund shouts from behind.

"Add your bonus to the tab." The man nods and walks away. I close the door and take the tray into my room. When I get inside the bed is empty. I look around and Daler is no longer in his place. I set the tray down and peek into the bathroom. I see steam forming and I assume he is in the bath. I walk over and pull the curtain back. He has his eyes closed and his head is leaned back, resting. I bend toward him and rub my fingers through his hair.

"Ummm. That feels nice." He moans.

"I have food for us in the room."

"You know we have to go back." He says. His voice sounds sad.

"I know. I am ready when you are."

"I will never be . . . ready. But we have to leave tonight. My father called and he wants me back in two days."

"Why?"

"Because Ciria has moved to Jutesh and she not only signed the treaty she has relinquished control over to me."

"You? Not your father?"

"She elected me as the new leader over Mochatson. Father wants me to combine it with Jutesh."

"I understand."

"Join me." he says as he lightly pulls at my robe. I untie it and it drops to the floor. I step in and lie on top of him.

When we finish our bath, sit on the bed and eat. We laugh and enjoy our last day in Shashburg. Emund steers clear of us the rest of the day. I dress and pack for the return to Jutesh. I have to admit, I am saddened that we have to leave. Our affection will have to be more discreet. Khattris cannot get a notion that I have given myself to Daler. I will not lose the future I have ensured with him.

"Are you ready to leave this place?" Daler asks when he emerges from the room dressed.

"No, but I know what I have to do."

"I promise we will still have this when we return."

"We will have to be careful and more discreet."

He sighs. "Do not worry about my father Chakori."

"I cannot help myself. He will kill me." He walks over to me and pulls me to him.

"We will be married in 53 days. Concentrate on counting them down, nothing else. Alright?"

I nod my head in agreement. *53 more days and I will not have to worry about Khattris any longer.* I have been so absorbed in life here I had forgotten about my life of a dignitary in Jutesh.

"Let's go."

We exit the penthouse hand-in-hand and meet Emund at the elevators. We proceed down to the vehicle that awaits us. We arrive to the plane just before dark. We board and settle in our seats. Before we have to buckle ourselves in, Daler comes over to where I am sitting and renders me one last bout of public affection. He kisses me softly and sensually on my lips and runs his hands through my loose hair. He caresses it and returns to his seat. Emund looks in on us to make sure we are comfortable before the plane soars into the sky carrying us back to the island of lies and scandal.

When our plane lands, there are plethora of people waiting for us.

Khattris is the lead of the entourage. He stands beside the plane with his fists clinched together. The door slides open and Daler steps off first. Emund takes hold of my arm and we follow.

I grasp at his arm for dear life. I begin to shiver. My fear has return at the sight of Khattris' face. I feel as if he sees right through me. My virtue is gone, perched high above the clouds. I am not sorry, the time I spent with my sweet Daler will forever keep me. I slowly step forward. With each stride I draw closer to my terror.

Daler confidently embraces his father. He smiles a hideous grin. The sight of this man puts a foul taste in my mouth. Daler steps aside. He opens his arms wide and waves for me to enter into them. I release Emund's arm and cautiously steps toward him. He hugs me and bile threatens to exit at the feel of his skin. His cheek grazes mine. I endure the sting of his prickly beard. He grabs my shoulders and searches my face with his eyes.

I stare back at him careful not to appear nervous. *The likeness between him and Daler are uncanny. I do not know how I could completely adore one and hate the other*. But it was not that long ago that I despised Daler the same. I smile and he releases me from his grip. He turns and places his arm around Daler. He winks at me, I blush. With just a gesture of his eye he has me weak at the knees. I grab ahold to Emund once more and we head home to the Khattris mansion.

Daler exits the vehicle first. Khattris follows. Emund bends and as he gets out. He reaches for my hand.

Chronicles of a Betrothed

I grab hold and step out. I look at the mansion and sigh as I enter the fortress that is my prison. When I get to my room, I close the door and prop myself against it. I take a deep breath and walk toward my luggage. Emund brought it up. I stopped in the main dining room to speak with Jasmine and Jasleen. I do not know why it seems that everyone knows of our trysts. I am waiting for someone to shout out, "We know what you two were doing while you were away." I would absolutely die, literally. I unpack and put away my things. I pick up my gown and remember the evening two nights ago. I hold it close and remember how he revealed he really loved me and how he would not be without me. He promises to protect me. I think about his lips on my ankles and it is heaven. I want to be there again. But that is not an option right now. We cannot risk getting caught. I sigh as I hang the gown in my closet. My wardrobe has dramatically changed in the last months. I know dress like the wife of a modern ruler. My tunics and long beaded skirts seem silly now. As I change my traveling attire I slip into a comfortable dress I purchased in the UC. I turn in the mirror. I admire my new look. I hear a knock at the door.

"May I come in Chakori?" Jasleen asks as she pushes the door slightly open and peek in. She smiles as she spots me in the mirror.

"Hello Jasleen."

"I missed you. It was so boring. I wanted to tell you when we spoke down stairs. Jasmine has been very agitating. I will be glad when she leaves. Because now I have you."

"Thank you. I missed you. Your brother has taken me on a ride I never want to forget. I am ecstatic, but sad the trip had to end. The United Countries was very interesting. I have never witnessed so much technology. I was given a chance to see how people truly live. I hope one day to do the same. And to think Jasmine will get to live there for a while. I am jealous."

"Do not be. It will be all work and no play. I am very surprised you were able to have any. Daler is not usually so loose."

"He was occupied with President Hunter. I did not see him until the last day."

"Oh, I see."

"Emund takes very good care of me."

"Alright. Well did you hear about Monarch Rykii's daughter joining us?"

"Of course I did. I do not like it."

"Why? She looks like she could be your sister. Really you guys look very much alike."

"I know. But she has been very flirtatious with Daler."

"Yes. She is very interested in him. She expressed to our father she is willing to lead our lands by his side, should your arrangement fail." I gasp. She is not even here a month and she is striking very quickly.

Jasleen notices the terror in my eyes. "Do not worry Chakori. You are the promised one not her."

"I know. But . . ." I turn away so I do not reveal my secrets. I love Daler and if Ciria gets wind of our physical interactions. I will die and she will be his bride. And even if I do not die, I will never live with that scenario.

"What is this? Do I detect a bit of jealousy? Do you actually care for Daler?"

"Oh I . . . just . . ."

Chronicles of a Betrothed

"Chakori!! Are you falling for my brother?"

I run to the door and look out of it. I close it and lean against it.

"Shhhh! Jasleen. You are talking entirely too loud." I walk over to the bed and sit.

"I must admit even the most sadistic person can have a certain kind of charm."

"Please quiet your voice Jasleen. I do not want your father to find out."

"Find out what? That you actually like your evil tyrant husband to be?"

"Yes, he may mistake it for something else."

"Do not worry, I will not say a word."

I sigh. I lie back and cover my eyes. I haven't had many friends. My father never really trusted anyone. So I have the need to express my love for Daler to someone.

"Jasleen I need you to keep our conversations confidential." She hurries over to me and sits beside me on the bed.

"I've fallen for him. He is the most interesting person I know. And, he actually loves me back."

"How do you know?"

"He revealed it to me when were together at the President's dinner. I was floored and realized that he was slowly getting inside my heart. Spending those days with him on the plane permitted me to see a different side of him. He is a gentle man to the ones he cares for."

"Ha! He is just like his father and you will find out. I know you did not ask for this but you have fallen in love with a terrible person. I am so sorry Chakori."

"I will be fine. I need sleep I have been traveling and I am absolutely exasperated. We will talk another time. Is that alright?"

"Yes, fine then. I will catch up with you when you are well rested. We have not had the pleasure of touring the island together."

"I promise we will get a chance to do whatever you like." She gives me a smirk and exits the room. I take off my dress and prepare for bed. I find a white night gown I purchased while visiting Shashburg. I bathe and slide into it. I turn out my light and wrap myself in my covers. I start to drift when my door opens. I try and focus on who it could be, but when they do not say a word I figure it is my husband to be. He slides beside me.

"I had to come and bid you a goodnight."

I turn to meet him. I feel the warmth of his breath hit me as I face him. "I am so glad you came to me. I am going to go mad not having the freedom to see you when I please."

"You can see me whenever wish. If you call I will come. I promise." He wraps me in his arms and carefully kisses my lips. I cradle his face in my hands and return the affection.

"Daler," I say breathing into his face. "I am so happy to be here with you. My feelings for you are so strong they haunt me when you are not near. I do not know how and why but I am the happiest I have ever been, even though I am living here under the roof with a mad man."

He smiles and I can see all of his teeth in this dim dark room. His grin incapacitates me. "Which one of us is the mad man?"

Chronicles of a Betrothed

I cannot help but chuckle at the irony. He is correct, they are both men that handle things with a notion of using any means necessary.

"I will not answer that."

He kisses the tip of my nose. We pull one another closer and hold each other tighter. He breathes into my face. I can hear the frustration in his sigh.

"Please dream of me sweet Chakori, I assure you I will only have thoughts of you swimming through the depths of my mind tonight." He releases me and, too soon he disappears. I snuggle into the covers and comply with my beloved's wishes.

My slumber is a lengthy one. When I awake it is well past midday. I wonder why no one has come to waken me. I jump from my bed, truly refreshed. I guess I really needed the rest. Every vision in my head that evening was of Daler. We were together, making love as we desired. No one could interrupt. I was his wife. I wish we could do it now. Just marry in the moment. I stretch my hand out in front of me and stare at the promise he made to me. No one had to make him do it. He wanted to. And, I am overwhelmed with glee. I stagger to the bathroom to bathe. I am intoxicated by the very essence of him. I dress and wonder from my room. The emptiness of the mansion concerns me. I walk down the hall tracing the lining of the wall with my finger. I am not in a hurry to be anywhere. I wonder where Emund is. He is always present. *What is different today?* I slowly walk down the stairs. I lazily step down each stair. When I reach the bottom I make my way to the dining room. There is not a soul present. I start to call out.

Annetta Hobson

"Hello?" No one answers. Maybe they are gone for the day. I smile at the thought of my love. He is all that is on my mind. I refuse to give my thoughts to anything or anyone. When I prepare myself to scream hello again I hear a muffled sound. It appears to be voices. I am never in the right place in this house. I travel toward the noise. I hear the voice of woman. She is panting. I get closer. Is someone being hurt? I pick up the pace. When I get to the door, I am at the main dining hall. I peek very carefully around the corner. I see Ciria naked propped onto the table. I grab my mouth. I cannot see the man she is with but I do not stay to find out. I run as fast as I can back to my room. I do not stop until I am there. When I arrive I shut the door quietly and lock it. I am drenched with worry. *Who was that? And where is everyone?* I go into my bathroom and throw water into my face so I do not faint. *Oh goodness, who could that be? Who is she with? And why were they out in the open like that?* I sit on my bed and cover my face. *What is going on?* I do not understand. I sit there for a moment and I hear a knock at my door. "Yes?"

"Open the door Chakori it's me." I smile it is Daler. I run to the door and swing it open. He stands there looking very handsome. His hair is wet and curly. His shirt is slightly unbuttoned. It appears as if he has been running. I reach to embrace him and he pushes me away.

"I'm so sorry. I am very sweaty."

I smile.

"I do not care. I want to touch you. Come in." I look outside of my door and the hall is still bare.

"How long have you been awake?"

"A few minutes why?"

Chronicles of a Betrothed

"Did you just get dressed?"

"Yes? What's wrong Daler?"

"Nothing. I will see you later."

Before I can embrace him he exits the room. I go to follow and Emund stops me.

"Good afternoon Mistress. Did you sleep well?"

"Yes . . ." I whisper. I am so confused right now. I do not know what has occurred.

"Let us go and eat." I give him a puzzled look.

"Where were you?"

"I was asked to take the women out."

"Lady Surina, Jasmine and Jasleen?"

"Yes mistress. Is there something wrong? Because I was instructed to let you sleep. Your betrothed came to wake you but you would not budge. They figured you were exhausted from the plane ride. So I was commanded to let you sleep."

"Was Monarch Khattris and Daler with you?"

"No mistress."

My heart sinks. I am shattered from the inside out. *Who was with Ciria? Who was making love to her blatantly for anyone to see? Anyone meaning me!* I stagger to the bed. My beloved was here. He was drenched with sweat, his shirt torn open a little. I clutch my chest as I hit the bed.

"Go Emund go!"

"What about lunch? You are being summoned."

"Tell them I am tired. I will not be joining them today."

"At all?"

"I afraid so. Not at all."

"As you wish Mistress? I will let everyone know." He turns to go. Sadness touches his eyes. He recognizes the hurt in my eyes. He knows Daler has stomped my heart. I grab the post of the bed to stand. I am weak. I feel as if I will die. <u>What happened? He loves me. He loves me, right</u>? Here come the tears, always there to betray me. I need to remain calm but my eyes will not comply. The tears run down my cheek. Did she penetrate the wall my beloved said only I could? Or was the whole venture a façade. I am utterly destroyed. *Is my Daler a liar? Just like his father. He does not love me. He uses those who are vulnerable and ravishes them that allow him. And like an imbecile I adhered to his every command.* I weep at my inability to recognize a ruse. I am forever tainted. No man will ever marry a soiled woman, a desecrated bride. I might as well die. I lie down. My tears soak the pillow. I don't even try to conceal it. I let my affliction be heard throughout the halls of the Khattris' mansion.

Chapter 13

I weep well into the night. Not a soul bothers to disturb my cry. The next morning is the same. I am there with no one to love me. I am back where I began. Except I no longer hold on to Elliot. I do not deserve his sacrifice. I gave myself to a man who loves nothing and no one. I wail. I still love him. I love him even more. *Why?* I hear a tapping on my door.

"Come in!" I hear a whiny giggle.

"Nice room Chakori of Ghatlan."

I sit up and look to her.

"That is Chakori of Jutesh! Ciria."

She steps toward me. I must admit. She looks beautiful. She is my image duplicated. Her hair is shiny and has curls. She has been enjoying the perks of this island. I scan her over. She is not the raggedy dirty wreck she was the day we visited her island.

"I must admit, I have been dying to see the inside of your quarters. I am impressed. The men of Jutesh do know how to care for a woman.*"*

I wipe my eyes and stand. "What do you want? Why are you here! Emund!!!" I yell but he does not answer.

"Oh my . . ." She answers in her thick island tongue. "He is not here. He is busy with important people and things." She frowns as if she feels bad for me.

"Do you really want to know what I am here regarding? I know you have an idea Chakori."

"Daler?" I answer. My voice barely able to squeeze his name out.

"Yes! I want all of him not just part of him. I am also territorial." She rubs her hip and her eyes close as if she is remembering a sensual moment. She laughs and exits my room.

I yell out for her to come back but she strolls down the hall and sashays down the stairs with not even as much as a glance. She is confident and strong. She is no longer pure. Daler has given her the same confidence I received. I slam my door. I run to bathe and dress. I will not go down like this. I want answers now! I make my way to the garden area outside. The family is sitting out there enjoying the mid-morning sun. They are eating and talking in hushed voices.

"Good morning everyone." I proclaim. Monarch Khattris looks to me first.

"Good morning, nice of you join us now sit." He points his fork toward the seat across from him.

Soon my eyes meet Daler's. He stands to greet me, his smile ever so wide. I scowl. He steps out from in front of his chair. When he reaches for my hand, I do not take it. I stomp pass him and sit. One of the maids run to me and asks me if I would like to eat. I nod and she scurries away.

Khattris grimaces. He drops his fork and wipes his mouth.

Chronicles of a Betrothed

"Now I have been very patient with you Chakori. But . . . you have skipped meals for a day since your return. Now you come to join us with a bit of rude manners. My son does not deserve that treatment from the likes of you." The thunder in his tone does not frighten me today. I slowly look to him.

"Please excuse me Monarch Khattris. I have been polite with your son. But he does not return the gesture." I hear a harmony of gasps with forks clinging on the plates. Khattris stands.

"From where has this mannerism come?" He moves around the table and everyone starts to leave.

Daler stands to meet his father. "Father it is alright. I will handle it."

"Obviously you cannot or she would have not treated you this way."

The garden is now evacuated. There is only Daler, Ciria, Monarch Khattris and me.

"Father." He says with authority. But Khattris does not care. He storms toward me. I brace myself for the coming infraction. I hold my head up high. I glance over and Ciria is smiling at the other end of the garden.

Khattris shoves Daler aside.

He attempts to grab his father.

"I think you have taken my hospitality as some sort of weakness. I do not care about the marriage. You can be replaced." He looks to Ciria and my eyes water.

"I do not care about it either. I have experienced love with Daler and I welcome death. I love him still even after deception. So give Ciria to him. He has defiled her also . . ."

Daler' eyes grow large. "Chakori! What are you saying?"

Annetta Hobson

"I saw the two of you yesterday. You made love to her like you did with me! And I do not care if your father kills me. The pain in my heart is far worse than any pain your father can inflict upon me!"

"Oh my dear, I doubt that!" Khattris grabs my arm and storms toward the house. He waves for Ciria to join. The smile has completely vanished from her lips. She jogs to keep up. Daler follows in a panic. He slides his hands through his hair and grabs at his beautiful locks to yank them. He is livid.

"What have you done Chakori?" he whispers to me as his father drags me along,

"I love you Daler and you betrayed me!" I scream as his father snatches me down the hall and to the basement where he killed Eveleen's brother. Fear strikes me. I turn to Daler and tears have set in his eyes. He mouths to me.

"Why?" I shake my head. He is trying to get there and I refuse to allow it.

Khattris opens the door of his killing room and pushes me in. He, Daler, and Ciria follows me in.

I run to the wall and cling to it. My heart is shattered into pieces. I no longer have to live. I will soon join Elliot and not even he will have me now.

Khattris approaches me. He walks so slowly he is moving like a wild animal stalking prey. "I asked you to remain pure until your wedding day."

"Father!"

"Quiet Daler! I told you I would kill you. My instructions are never to be ignored."

Chronicles of a Betrothed

Ciria stands in a corner closest to the door that Khattris has now locked.

"My son. Why did you not follow my instructions? Not only did you defile this bride. You entered them both! What is wrong with you? You are ruining everything we have worked for."

"First father, allow me to explain." He nods and Daler proceeds.

"I do not know what the hell is happening. I have not touched Ciria."

"Then why is she saying this?"

"I don't know father." he looks to me completely befuddled.

"I saw the two of you in the dining room yesterday. I did not see you but I saw her naked on the table."

She gasps and folds her arms.

"And when you came to my room perspiring, you treated me differently. I asked you what was it and got nothing. Your hair was wet and . . . she came to my room and basically confirmed it."

His eyes grow dark. He turns to Ciria and there is a dangerous look about his face.

"I . . . I did not say anything of the sort." She stutters.

"It does not matter. You, Chakori are not leaving this room alive."

I swallow hard. I knew it would come to this. I am about to die. At least Daler shows remorse for what he has caused.

Khattris pulls his gun from his waist. I close my eyes, I will join Elliot by the same weapon and same hand.

"NO!" Daler shouts.

I open my eyes and Khattris looks to him.

Annetta Hobson

"I will do it. My way."

His father hands him his weapon. Daler walks over to a table and set it down. His father stands in front of me. "I make the rules here sweet Chakori. My son's awful need for you just ended your worthless life."

I do not cry, this man does not deserve my tears. At least Daler has the kindness within to let me die fast. If left to Khattris I would be tortured.

Daler approaches me. "I have not touched anyone since the day I lay eyes on you Chakori. How could you think I would betray you, with her?" he points to Ciria. He pulls the knife from his ankle. He leans in and plants a lingering kiss on my forehead. "I love you more than anything and anyone." Tears stream down his cheek. "I will never ever love another."

I am speechless. How could I have betrayed his trust?

"One thing before I die, where were you coming from then? You were out of breath and your clothes were in disarray."

"My father and I had to take of something . . . someone. I did not want to tell you. I know you hate that side of me. I was trying to protect you from that."

My head falls, I feel like a fool. I have ended my life with a tale. Something I made up in my head, with the help of Ciria. I give her menacing look. I turn back to Daler and my hearts breaks at the sight of his lovely face. He grabs my head and embraces it. He rubs my hair while kissing my cheek. He twirls the knife in his hand which hangs at his side. Tears fall from his eyes onto my face.

"Enough Daler! Do it now! I want it over. I have to come up with a story for the people. You must have a pure bride. I have to make several decisions quickly. So just do it!"

He does not budge. His lips are still pressed firmly to my cheek. He cups the back of my head.

"Daler!" Khattris yells. Daler turns and Khattris gets closer.

"If you cannot do this I will." He squeezes through his teeth. Khattris reaches for the knife and Daler plunges it deep into his chest. Rage replaces sorrow.

Ciria screams through her fingers clutched over her mouth.

"I will not kill the only person who has ever truly seen through the murderous animal you designed me to be. I hate you Father for what you have forced me to do!"

Khattris grabs him with one hand and slides down his leg clutching his chest with the other.

My eyes are bulging from my head. I cannot scream.

Khattris begins to gasp for air. The expression of betrayal on his face is an awful sight to witness. He is killed by the one person he trusts. Many men have wanted to do what his beloved son has just done.

Daler wipes his tears. He watches as the breath leaves his father. He kicks his father's hand that is still attached to his leg. The life drains from his eyes along with the pool of blood surfacing beneath the body.

I grab my mouth. All I can do is gawk at Khattris as he dies.

Ciria is afraid to move. Her screams fade her breathing slows. She does not know what will come next.

Truthfully, I am awaiting the same. I look to the man who just murdered his father for me. And I feel responsible. *Why could I* have just not opened my mouth? How will he recover from this? "Daler my love?"

He doesn't answer. He stands over the body of his dead tyrant father. This was the most loathed man around the world. President Hunter hated his impulsiveness. I wonder how he would receive the news of the dead tyrant who agreed to execute his master plan of combining the islands under their one world government laws.

I call to him once more. "Daler?" I reach for his hand and grab the knife that he carries everywhere his fine shoes land. He does not refuse me when I pull the bloody blade from his tightly gripped fingers. He drops to his knees and lie atop of his father's lifeless body. I hear the door open and Ciria darts out. He looks at her and his head falls back to his father's corpse. I instantly take off after her. She does not get far before I jump her like a wild cat. I drag her back to the room still holding Daler's hunting knife.

We sit there for hours.

Ciria is crouched in the corner of the room weeping.

I stand at the door hoping and praying no one is searching for us. I peek from the room every now and then.

Daler is a mess. It is unnerving to see such a man in this state. I walk over to him I bend down to him and ask. "What should we do now?"

He looks to me and grabs my shoulder. He stands holding on to me.

"I told you I would never let anyone hurt you Chakori. I meant every word. Do you see now?"

Chronicles of a Betrothed

I feel sorrow. He should not have had to kill his father. "Yes but I did not want this."

"It doesn't matter. He is better off." He looks at the corpse once more. He walks over to the wall close to the door and picks up a phone.

I look to Ciria who is torn into pieces. The beauty I once seen in her is a mere shadow. She cowers in the corner. I hate her for what she implied. She wanted me to think she slept with what is mine. I walk over to her. The knife is in my hand still dripping Khattris' blood. She stands as I approach. She holds her hands up in surrender.

"Please, please!"

"Who were you making love to in the dining room!" She looks to Daler who is still on the phone.

"Wait Chakori wait."

"Tell me now!"

"It was Khalil my guard." She sighs.

Daler watches from the other side of the room.

"I wish Khattris had killed you. Then Daler would be mine. I have dreamed about him many nights." She throws her chin toward my Daler.

Rage takes me.

Daler notices and sets the phone down. He walks over and gently grabs the knife from my hand.

Ciria smiles. He turns and looks at her.

She gives him a pleading look. "Daler I will not breathe a word of this to anyone I promise. I could make a better bride. I swear to you."

His eyes are hollow. He watches carefully as she speaks.

"Please let me prove this to you. You would not have had to resort to this treason for me. I would be quiet as mouse for as long as you order it. I have been trained to love a man. I can satisfy your every desire."

"From the day we met, you have caused great problems." He stares at her. It is as if he is looking through her. He grabs a handful of her hair and quickly without thinking, slices her throat. I gasp. He releases her and she falls to the floor. He throws the knife down beside her. The sounds of her gurgling immobilizes me.

"Why Daler? Why did you kill her?" I yell.

"Because if I didn't you would have. And I do not want you to ever experience that."

He walks back to the phone and picks it up. He pushes the button and begins to dial someone else.

"I need you down in the basement now! Yes, I have two. And, you have to be discreet." He hangs up the phone and ushers me from the room.

I look back to see Ciria, the woman I hate and Khattris, the man I detest, lying on the floor forever a memory in a horrible tale that I will not soon forget.

Daler rushes up the stairs pulling me behind him.

I stumble up each one trying to keep from falling. I wonder why he is so calm. As we reach the second floor of the mansion Emund is heading our way.

"I do not want anyone to know of this Emund. You have to totally destroy everything. Get rid of the room. Come and find me when it is done."

Emund nods. His eyes never connect with mine.

Chronicles of a Betrothed

I wonder what Daler will tell his mother. *How will she deal with the news that her husband is dead?* Questions swirl inside of my mind. I dare not ask. I have a little joy inside of me. I am not the one lying dead on the floor of the family's death room. When we reach my room Daler hurries in and locks the door.

"Take your clothes off my love." He turns to me and starts to undress me. At first I am confused, but I glance down at the blood soaked fabric. His clothes are stained as well. After I am undressed he follows. We stand in the middle of my bedroom naked.

"I am so sorry Chakori. I . . ." I place a single finger over his lips.

He stops midsentence, his lips partially parted.

"I am the one who should be apologizing Daler. I have caused you to commit the unthinkable. I was not aware the love we share is of this magnitude. Please know I will never doubt you again."

He smirks, but it quickly fades.

I am unsure of the thoughts traveling throughout his mind. I glare at his face. *He is such a beautiful creature. How could something so gorgeous be so vicious?*

"Let us clean up and then we will talk. Is that okay with you for now, love?"

I nod. I am a ball of nerves. Murderous tirades have become a part of my everyday life. He grabs my hand and we bathe. I dress in one of my evening gowns. It is not one of the fancy ones I own. I glide my hands along the fabric as I look in the mirror. Khattris specifically requested, no demanded I wear them. Though the very sight of him sickened me, I will wear this dress in his honor tonight. Daler emerges from the bath and he is wearing a towel. It is wrong for my thoughts to travel to this place right now but, I would love to lay down with him and thank him for saving my life. The way the water drips from his hair and lands on his muscular shoulder makes my soul dance. I watch as it slithers down his shoulder to his formed chest. It lingers at the hair on his chest before streaming down to the tip of the towel that is snugly wrapped around his waist.

"Did you know the very look you are giving me is the reason we are in this mess today?"

I shake my thoughts away. "What do you mean?"

"The first day I entered your room."

"I do not understand."

"When you were enjoying . . . well I was enjoying the sound of you enjoying yourself."

I flush bright red. He has a way of bringing the blood out of people. I just happen to still be alive.

"I just peeked from the bathroom."

"You watched me like a fine meal you wanted to devour."

"Impossible."

"Chakori." He says as he approaches. "You peered around the corner," he says. "And your eyes captured me. The way you looked at me rendered me helpless. I was unable to think of anything else."

I smile. He approaches me. I look to his hands that clutch the towel. Slowly he unravels it. I am glued in place. Suddenly there is a banging at my door. I jump. He tucks his towel in and unlocks it. Emund stands there and he is panicked. He steps in and Daler shuts the door behind him.

Chronicles of a Betrothed

"Sir . . ." He pauses to catch his breath. He bends to grip his knees. "It is done. I have disposed of the bodies completely. They will never be discovered."

"Are you sure?"

"I am absolutely positive sir. There is nothing left to find. I am going now to clean the room and furnish it. No one will ever know what is used for."

"I do not want details, especially in front of Chakori." He places a hand on Emund's shoulder. "Thank you dear friend. You are a great asset."

"Are you going to be alright sir?"

Daler grimaces.

Emund accepts that as his answer and exits.

"I will be right back. Do not leave." He stares into my eyes to make sure I am clear of his instructions.

I blink uncontrollably before nodding in agreement. He leaves the room in a flash with the towel still wrapped around his fine body. I sit on the bed to reflect day's tragic events. I cannot believe that Pavan Khattris is dead. *I really wanted Ciria to die after what she did to me. But no one deserves death I guess. What am I saying?* I think. *This mansion of death is taking its toll on me. I love Daler and the fact that he is a murderer is no longer a concern of mine. I have witnessed his crimes and I still feel the same about him.* I sit there for a while. Soon I hear a tap on the door.

He peeks in and smiles. He acts as if his father is not dead and buried in some unknown place, if he is even buried. It is not known where Emund has stashed them.

Annetta Hobson

It is no burden I will carry. When he steps in he looks dashing. I know that he has the finest taste in clothing.

"Come beautiful we have something we need to do." He extends his hand toward me. I smile and take hold. I am living in his world and there is nowhere else I would rather be. We walk down the stairs. I step carefully. Since I have been in Jutesh, I only wear high heeled shoes. I am used to them now but I still use caution. I look to the dining area before we leave out of the mansion. First Lady Surina is sitting at the table eating alone. She waves to me. Guilt floods my belly, but I manage a giddy return. Daler pulls me toward the luxurious vehicle that awaits us. I am so in awe with him. I believe love has found me once again. I will treasure every waking moment this time. "Where are we going?"

"You ask too many questions. Let me have this day. I promise I will never disappoint you."

I beam at his words. I believe him and I leave this life of mine securely in his hands.

We arrive at a wonderfully constructed building. It resembles the restaurants in the UC. Daler steps out and grabs my hand. Emund is not accompanying us this evening. The reason is obvious. I wrap myself around his arm and walk alongside him into the building. The doors open and I am blown away. It is much more than anything I witnessed in Shashburg. The aroma of the brightly lit candles hit me and I instantly forget about everything else.

"Do you like it?"

"I love it. What is this?"

Chronicles of a Betrothed

"I wanted to take you out of that house. This is the best place for that." I scan the room and there are servers standing in place waiting for instructions.

"I have been planning this since our return. Today's events threatened to ruin it but I felt you needed it anyway." He grabs my hand tight and lifts it to his lips. We proceed to a table in the middle of the room. I am too happy. I should feel angst but I do not. I feel nothing but love and ease. Pavan cannot hurt me.

He slides the chair out for me to sit. I slowly sit. He walks around the table, I watch his every movement. He is mine and mine alone. We share more than stolen sensual moments. We now share hearts. The evening is like a dream or a snippet from a storybook. We eat and drink until I am barely able to hold my eyes open. We talk but not about the horror we experienced. I want to forget and my love is creating a fine distraction.

Daler stands and walks around the table. He extends his hand and look toward a man playing a string instrument. "Will you please dance with me?" He asks in his most sensual persuading tone.

Although I am extremely tired, I will not turn down an invitation to touch bodies with the man who just hours ago committed a heinous and unheard of deed for me. "I would love to Daler." I blink slowly as I stand. A yawn escapes.

"Are you tired?"

"I am, but I want one dance with you."

He smiles and assists me to the middle of the floor. He twirls me around with his hand like a music box doll. I spin and land snuggly into his arms. He grabs my hands and places them around his neck. My hands graze his curls. I steal a feel. I quickly run my

Annetta Hobson

fingers through his silky hair. He shuts his eyes and indulges in the exchange. He places his hands on my back. I allow my head to fall onto his chest and we start to move slowly rocking to the sweet rhythm coming from the instruments. I remove my hands from his neck and slide them underneath his arms to hug his chest.

"I want you to forget what you saw today. I do not want it to haunt you." He whispers into my hair.

It is a little late for this request. The death of Pavan will haunt me forever. "I will try. I have never witnessed the countless acts shown to me since my arrival. I will be forever grateful to you for your sacrifice. So I will work hard to put today out of mind."

"I will always protect you. No matter whom it may be. You are my family now and no one will ever hurt you. And if there is a time when someone tries, they will suffer the same fate as those before them." He cups my face between his gentle murderous hands.

I lift my eyes to his. They penetrate my soul. He holds my face. I lay my hands atop of his. He leans in to touch my lips with his. We stop dancing to lose ourselves in one another. I passionately kiss his soft lips. I want to be in him. I crave his touch. And he is satisfying my inner want. Finally he releases me. My eyes remain closed.

"I love you Chakori. You own my heart, please handle it with care. It is not accustomed to so much emotion." His eyes search mine as I think of a reply.

"I love you. I will love you forever. I will do my best to never disappoint you. I am awakened now that I have you." He smiles my wonderful smile. I push my face back into his chest and he rests his chin in my hair. We dance until my strength leaves me.

Chronicles of a Betrothed

He pulls me away and wraps his arm around my shoulder. He nods to the servers. We exit the building and enter the car.

We leave to return home and I could not have enjoyed him more. On the drive home he holds me in his arms. I snuggle in and inhale the scent of the man that makes my life worth living.

Chapter 14

About a month and a half has past. In two weeks I will marry the man I love. I sit up in my bed, smiling at how things have changed. Pavan's absence has everyone on edge. Daler knows he will have to do something soon. I on the other hand am on cloud nine. The threat of death no longer lingers over my head. My days are filled with Daler's presence. He showers me with gifts. Things I could have never known existed now adorn my wardrobe. I have jewels finer than any. I love my life. Daler's murdering antics are fading. He is the calm man I long for him to be. All of my evenings are ignited with the anticipation of him slipping in and making love to me. He does things to my body that should not be lawful, and I welcome it. I close my eyes and wish for his company. When I open them to stand, I grab hold to the bed post. My head is spinning. Thoughts of my husband to be have me in a spiral. I sit to see if the feeling will dissipate. But I move to quickly and bile rises from my belly. I run to the bathroom. I heave into the toilet bowl. I instantly bind my hair in a knot. I try and reach for a towel but it gives me no rest. I feel as if I am giving my insides to the gods of the latrine. I finally finish my bout with my queasy stomach. I rise and Daler is standing in my bathroom doorway.

"Are you alright Chakori?" He rushes to me and helps me stand.

"I must be coming down with something. No need to be alarmed." But for some reason my words do not soothe him.

"I am calling Eveleen now!" he storms from my room. I start to follow but the commode calls me back. I give up all of the food that lies within. I lie there a moment clutching my temporary comforter. Daler returns and his worry has grown.

"There is a sickness going around the island. I hope you have not caught it. A young girl died last week."

"Oh Daler you are overacting. I am sure it was the shellfish from last night. Do not worry."

"I have not come this far to lose the only thing I live for."

I smile I want to kiss him. But I am sure he would rather not.

He helps me up from the floor. We slowly make our way to the bed. I feel my knees beginning to buckle. I place my hand over my forehead.

"Yes my love, you are perspiring." I wipe it once more and glance at my hand.

"I am just a little warm that is all."

"I will let Dr. Agroia decide that."

Just as I lie down the door opens.

"I think I have a potential patient here." Eveleen says as she enters.

"I am fine, Daler is just anxious."

"He should be. There is a terrible virus going around the island, if untreated death has been the result." She says with concern.

"Well with that being said let's get started." I say as I turn to Daler who is now out of his mind. He leans close to my ear and whispers.

"I did not go through what I went through just to lose you. I will not accept that." He lifts and speaks to Eveleen. "I know you must hate me. But please help my bride."

"I am a professional Khattris. Something you missed about me." She sarcastically spits.

He purses his lips. "No something my father missed. And as you see he is not here."

"I see he is not here but I know he is not far away, so I will get to your ailing bride to be." She turns to me and takes out her tools. She checks my temperature and listens to my chest.

"I will have to draw blood." She takes out a needle and I hold out my arm. I close my eyes and the pain from the puncture surges through my vein.

"I want to try one other test before I go." She removes a white devise from her bag. It is electronic. She pulls it apart and it is only connected by a cord.

"Lift your night shirt." I anxiously look to Daler. He notices my alarm.

"Wait Agroia! You do not have to give her an exam."

"I want to listen to her stomach." She states a bit annoyed.

"Alright?" He returns confused. Shortly after she places the device over my stomach, I hear a muffled rhythm of sounds. The sound immolates a thunderous heartbeat. Her eyes quickly shoot in horror to Daler. She drops the device and grabs his arm.

My eyes widen, she will surely die approaching him in that manner.

They cross the room in a hurry. They exchange words and finally Daler is quieted. His eyes grow wide. He looks to me and covers his mouth. He massages his beard and they return to me.

"How long have you been feeling this way love?" Daler says trying to calm himself. I look between them in confusion.

"I do not know . . . maybe a couple of days. But I only purged today."

Eveleen steps up and grabs my hand. "Chakori my dear you are pregnant. I am certain of it. I will still run some tests on your blood. But I need you to come to my office for an ultrasound."

"Pregnant, no!" I look over to Daler. His expression has changed from anxious to serious.

"Now Eveleen you know what this means? We need to be very discreet."

"I know." She sighs. "Bring her to my office after dark. All of my workers will be gone."

"If you breathe a word of this I . . ."

"Young Khattris, there is no need to threaten me. I am well aware of the consequences of crossing your family." She packs her bag and turns back to me.

"You have nothing to worry about. I will take care of you." She rolls her eyes at Daler and exits my room.

"What are we going to do Daler? I will be a disgrace if this gets out. My father . . ."

Chronicles of a Betrothed

"Have you forgotten my love? I am in charge now, in more ways than you can imagine. We will be fine. We have to marry now." He grabs my hand and I sit upward.

"We are to marry in two weeks."

"No we will marry the day after tomorrow. I will make the plans. I have some things to prepare. Get dressed now love, we leave shortly."

I swing my legs to the side of the bed and stand. Immediately I am light headed. *What will we do if anyone gets wind?* I rush around getting dressed. The thought of carrying Daler child strikes me. I am suddenly overcome with happiness. My belly is filled with the love that Daler and I share.

Daler drives to Eveleen's office. In all of the months I have spent with him I have never witnessed this. I guess the delicateness of this situation calls for total secrecy. We reach her office and he slides a hood over my head. I pull it over my eyes. I can barely see. We enter and he surveys the area to check for witnesses. Eveleen meets us and ushers us to a room. The door reads "Exam room." We step in and there are several machines there. She immediately gets started. I lie down on the table she points to, lift my blouse and she covers my belly in a clear squishy liquid. She places the extension from the machine on my belly and I immediately spot the child. I can see it like I am looking through glass. It is so beautiful. I have a window through to my stomach. Daler laughs. It is the most joyous sound I have heard from his mouth.

"She is approximately three months. You two are going to be the parents of twin babies. Her abdomen is going to be growing quickly. She is beginning to show now. I look down and she is correct. I suspected weight gain, but I assumed it was from the fine eating I have enjoyed.

"Two babies? I could not have asked for anything better. We wed day after tomorrow."

Eveleen looks to the floor.

Daler is alarmed by her silence.

"I made some calls before we left the mansion notifying President Hunter of the wedding. Your father will be brought over."

I nod. I am afraid to speak.

He mows Eveleen over with his eyes. "Do we have a problem Agroia?"

"No Daler we do not." She folds her arms.

"I am so sorry but I do not believe you."

"I do not know what to say. But I assure you there is no problem." He glares at her and exits.

"Please do not let him kill me Chakori. I beg of you." I wipe my stomach and sit up. She begins to pace the room. I watch her in silence.

"He is going to kill me I know it."

"No Dr. Agroia." I approach her and I grab her hand to pull her close to me.

"He has changed. His father forced him to be that way. He no longer wants to do those things. You will be fine." I hug her to ensure her survival.

"He does not deserve a woman like you Chakori. Ciria would be a better match. Evil runs through her veins. Their union would make sense. He will destroy you. Please do not trust him."

Chronicles of a Betrothed

I squeeze her hands. "I know he loves me Eveleen. I have seen his love with my own eyes."

Tears surface and she is as vulnerable as a small animal.

But I know what he has done for me. I just cannot disclose it to her. After time has passed I notice Daler has not returned. I release her hand and walk to the door. I peek into the hall. I spot Daler with Emund and two others. I step back and close the door. Fear strikes me; he is going to kill her. I look at her and she starts to sob.

"He cannot do this. You are the only physician I trust. I will not take another." She covers her mouth.

"Oh no! He is out there. What is happening?" She screams.

Sorrow takes me. I feel helpless. Eveleen has been through so much. I do not want her to die. I turn and Daler is opening the door. His expression is like stone.

"Come Chakori we are leaving." He grabs my hand and yanks me toward the door.

Eveleen is in the corner terror fills her eyes. "Please Daler. I will not tell. I promise." He stops and turns to her.

"I killed your brother. You provide for his widow and child. Would you not love revenge? If everyone found out about my children . . . you have everything you need to destroy what I have built. I will not let anyone stop me. I have come too far." He releases my hand and walks over to her.

"I killed Pavan he is dead. So I am the new leader of the islands. He wanted to take everything away from me. I am now on the threshold of having all that I long for. So I will not have you ruining that for me."

"What about President . . ."

Annetta Hobson

"On board with me. I will reveal my father's fate in due time. As for you Goodbye."

"Please? I want to live." She begs.

He is silent. He grabs the knob to the office door

I stand there. His callousness revolts me. I cover my mouth. He lied to me. I look to him and he does not look back. He pulls me forward to follow him. I want to say something but I don't know how he will respond. I swallow hard and open my mouth to speak.

"I do not wish to hear what you are thinking. I did not lie to you Chakori. After what I have done for you, you should never question my motives."

He is correct I should never question his motives. But how can he enjoy inflicting fear into people. I trot behind him as we turn the corner. He nods to Emund. He starts toward Eveleen's office. I imagine Eveleen's face. She is so beautiful. I do not want her to die, at least not today. I don't want another soul to put their hands on me.

"Daler." I whisper. My voice is hoarse. I clear my throat and say it louder. "Daler!" I stop in my tracks.

He attempts to yank me forward but does not put much effort.

"Chakori please come. We need to get you back to the mansion. You need lots of rest."

"I do not want her to die!"

"I will not discuss this with you. You promised to stay out of political affairs."

"This is not a political affair. I do not want anyone else caring for me. She is the only person to touch me besides you. I want her for the babies."

Chronicles of a Betrothed

He ponders. His eyes search my face. He tilts his head. I wait for a response. He reaches out, takes his thumb and gently slides it across my lower lip.

"Why are you doing this?"

"Doing what? I am new to this society. A physician is someone who is intimate. I will not take another." I fold my arms and return his intense stare.

"Alright." He sighs.

And just like that Eveleen lives? I cannot believe it.

He reaches up and caresses my loose locks. He extends his hand toward me. I unfold my clutched arms and take a hold of it. We walk back to the office.

When we reach the door one of the guards are outside the door. Daler waves and he steps aside. When he opens the door Eveleen is crouched in a corner and Emund is preparing to take care of her. She spots my horror fills my eyes.

I run to her.

She embraces me. "Oh God Chakori. Thank you for coming back for me." I turn to Daler and he places his hands into the pockets of his slacks.

She cries for a while.

"Sir?" Emund says.

"It is alright Emund, you may leave." He nods and they leave.

"Eveleen? Please thank my bride. But I promise if you betray me you will befall a fate worse than death."

"I promise I will never breathe a word. The whole incident is forgotten."

"It better be. And as insurance I will put a special detail on your lovely niece and sister in law."

"That is not necessary I assure you."

"No I insist. Besides you love to travel. We do not want you getting any ideas."

"Thank you Daler."

"No thank Chakori. If it were not for the fact that I cannot deny her requests that you live." Daler exits the office once more.

She turns her weary eyes to mine. "Thank you. I do not know what I have done to deserve your mercy but I am in your debt."

"I just want you to take care of me. Help me have the healthiest pregnancy possible."

"I will not let you down." I stand and pull her up beside me. She embraces me once more. I leave her in the office and hurry to catch my husband to be. When I reach him he is waiting at the end of the hall. I place a hand on his shoulder he turns to me and his eyes have softened.

"I am so sorry I interfered. I just would not be able to live knowing about her demise." He places his hands on my waist and pulls me close.

"I really thought I would be angry with you if you ever tried to control me but . . ." He turns his face away. I place my thumb and forefinger on his deliciously defined chin and bring his eyes to mine.

"But what Daler?"

"I love giving into you Chakori. Please do not take advantage of it."

I smile. *He is so charming. Even with the murderous bloodline he has inherited.* "I am the last person on earth that you should worry about taking advantage of you. I adore you Daler.

Chronicles of a Betrothed

Who could witness what I have and still be enchanted by the very thought of you."

He removes my hands and places them around him.

I take hold. I squeeze him tightly, I never want to let go. We kiss tenderly. *I want to live in moments like these. He is a gentle man in love, not the tyrant that has to install fear.*

As we kiss Eveleen exits her office and makes her way toward us. The shattered woman that lay there minutes ago preparing for death is gone. The professional woman has returned. As she passes she slides her hand across my back.

I watch her face and she offers a slight glint of a smile. It dissipates at the sight of my beloved.

"Goodnight Khattris." She states before disappearing out of the door.

"Let's go home Chakori." He wraps one arm around me to grip my growing belly and we walk to our vehicle.

Chapter 15

It is the morning of my wedding and I cannot focus. Tons of bodies enter and exit my room. Sweat threatens to ruin the whole plan. Not a single curl will stay in my hair. I cannot think of a one reason why I would be so nervous. This day is the very reason I am even here in Jutesh. The man who planned this is just not here to witness his evil plan in action. I stand from my bed and walk to the mirror. The undergarments they gave me are very sensual. I imagine what Daler will think of them when he undresses me later tonight. I walk to the window. I notice that the property is starting to crowd. I gaze at an abundance of fancy vehicles pulling in. I pat my chest. My nerves consume me. I hear a knock at my door.

"Come in." I look to the door and Jasleen enters. I inhale and step toward her.

"How do you feel?"

"I am fine. My nerves are just bothering me a bit."

"They should. You are about to be the pawn in a very evil plot. I know father will be here to finally witness his treaty agreement come to fruition."

Annetta Hobson

I nod. I know her father will not be attending. But what I do not know is how Daler is going to explain it. He has spread his father has been touring the United Countries, gloating about his new treaty agreements. I know people will be expecting him and Ciria's attendance.

"You look very pretty Chakori. My brother is very lucky to have such a bride. I did not know if you would be here after your behavior that day we last saw father, but here you are. Ciria surely wanted your place. I guess Father sent her back to Mochatson."

I try to put a smile on my face. I do not know if it fully forms. "Maybe?"

I turn to go over to my vanity station. I sit and Jasleen follows. "You are going to make a spectacular bride. I glide the lipstick across my lips. I press my hand over my already neatly fastened hair. I slip a big white flower into the bind. I clasp the jeweled luxurious necklace around my neck. I rise from my seat to go over to my dress.

"Why aren't the servants assisting you?"

"Oh, Daler said I did not have to have them."

"Alright. Daler acts as if he owns the place. He knows it is tradition for the bride to be prepared for her groom. It is no different than the introduction ball. Father will not be pleased."

I turn to her, slightly irritated. "Jasleen, Daler will be in charge. So if he sees fit to change things should he not have that right?"

She steps back. "I suppose."

I turn and grab my dress from the hook. It is a glamorous gown. It is as white as the clouds in the sky. It has the finest jewels. Much more expensive than the one I wore in the UC. I lift it and unzip it.

"May I help?"

"Of course."

She places it on the floor so I can step into it. We pull it up and I slide my arms in. I pull the straps over my arms. Then Jasleen starts to zip me in. When she gets midway the zipper stops.

"Have you gained weight?"

"Yes . . . a little." She yanks at the zipper it finally gives. I glare at my reflection and I love what it returns.

"You look wonderful!"

"Thank you Jasleen." I say as I hug her.

"I will go and wait for your entrance with the rest of the guest." She rubs my arm and then exits. As the door shuts behind her my mind travels back to Khattris. I shake off my thoughts and open my door. I lift my dress and proceed to the waiting area prepared for me. I carefully take each stair to my future. I am so excited to begin my legitimate life with my new husband.

I sit in the lounge waiting for the ceremony to start. I rest my freshly decorated face on my painted hands. I slide the ring off of my finger that Daler presented to me in the UC. It will soon be replaced by the actual wedding band. I smile at the thought of Daler kissing me in front of hundreds of people. All of the delegates of the treaty will be here, with the exception of the Rykii family. I close my eyes to deflect the thought of their demise. There is a tap on the door. I stand and open it. My father is here. He smiles when he lays eyes on me.

"Hello sweet daughter."

Annetta Hobson

"Father . . . hello." I do not share his elation. It is because of him I have had to witness murder after murder. He stretches his arms wide.

"Hug your father dear. I have missed you." I turn and take my seat.

"I understand your anger Kori. But this had to be done. We have had so much peace on the island since the treaty. Your mother is able to enjoy the outdoors as she has always desired."

"Well father that is the best part of this deal. Mother gets to go outdoors. I am so happy I cannot contain it." I roll my eyes.

He gasps. "Is that what they have taught you here? To disregard the love of your family?"

"I've learned nothing here father. As a matter of fact, I have been taught heartlessness and malice."

"I see." He holds his arm in the air. "It is time to present you to your betrothed."

"That is the best thing you have said since you entered Father." I take his arm and we step outside. We walk over to the building where the introduction gala had taken place.

My father does not look to me again. I must have angered him and I do not care. I walk with ease down the line of flowers. The room is different from the gala. I make eye contact with each onlooker. I am the center of the universe right now. Finally, I look to the head of the room and Daler is dressed in the finest suit ever seen on a man. My heart begins to flutter. All of the horrible things I have witnessed leave my mind. I am his and we are going to be a family, one better than either of us has. I free one of my hands from the bouquet of flowers and caress my growing abdomen. I smile and when I look up Eveleen is staring directly into my eyes. I smile at her, but she does extend the same courtesy. I wonder if things have changed. *Has her gratitude for me faded? I did not think she would hate me.* As we pass her I watch her eyes. All I see is anger. I turn from her and Daler notices her expression. He looks to Emund who is standing along the side of the aisles. Eveleen understands what that entails and her expression quickly brightens. I finally reach my prince and I am engulfed in his love. I release my father's arm without looking back. Daler takes my hand and I am drowning in a sea of emotions. The music chimes and I am embedded in this moment. I stare into the eyes of the man I have fallen madly in love with. Despite the circumstances I have love, reciprocated love and no one can separate us ever.

We exchange vows and the ceremony is over as swiftly as it started. Our kiss is so eternal I do not want it to end. The crowd erupts into applause. He pulls away from my affection. I will keep him there all day if I could. We are introduced and the entire gathering moves to the garden. I am beaming, I smile so brightly that those who approach me has to return. Surina walks over to us. My smile fades.

"Chakori, you are the loveliest bride I have ever seen. I cannot say I was as happy as you seem on my wedding day. I believe my son will be an excellent husband. I must apologize for Pavan. I do not know why he is not in attendance. You would assume that he would be here for the marriage he fought so hard to arrange."

"I am sure there is a legitimate reason." Before I can get into our conversation Daler whisks me away. I look to the entrance of the garden and President Hunter is entering with First Lady Melody. Daler rushes to meet him. I am firmly attached to him.

"I am so sorry to be the bearer of such terrible news." Hunter exclaims. Surina and his sisters join us.

"What is it Daler?" Surina states.

"I do not know mother. He was just about to speak." She clenches to Daler's free arm.

"First lady Surina." Hunter nods. She nods back. "As I was informing Daler, I have terrible news." She clutches her chest.

"I received a death threat about a week ago. I disregarded it. I was told if I had any dealings in the Islands of Amity treaty agreement I would be killed like Pavan. I knew he was in Bosimia. Then I received a delivery before our flight. I did not want to tell you such news over the phone." His guard hands him one of the boxes. I am bewildered. I do not understand what is happening.

Daler takes the box and when he opens it there is a hand in it with Khattris ring on the finger. I scream. I hear synonymous yelps as my eyes roll shut.

When I open my eyes there is hysteria unfolding. Eveleen is standing over me. She does not speak. I try to stand. My perfect day is no longer mine. I hear Daler and President Hunter talking. Surina has been taken away. Eveleen helps me to my feet. She leans in and whispers.

"Move slowly, you fainted."

I turn to look at her. "Thank you." She places my hand in Daler's and departs. "What is happening Daler?" I ask.

"Someone has killed my father and Ciria. They do not want this treaty to exist."

"Ciria how . . . what has happened?"

Chronicles of a Betrothed

"Ciria's head lay in the matching package. Somehow someone got wind of our plans. They most know that she signed Mochatson over to me. It must be one of the natives."

"But it is too late, correct? Who could do such a thing?"

"Yes First Lady Chakori. You are royalty now my dear.

I agree with Monarch Daler maybe a native of Mochatson." President Hunter states with confidence. "It is impossible to know at this moment. But we will do our best to help you find the murderer of the Monarch. Now I must go. My life may be in danger. My very presence is a threat to our lives."

"I understand." Daler shakes his hand.

"Let me know what your next order of business will be. I will await your notification. Be careful young Monarch, I fear for your life as well." He and his entourage disappear into the darkness of the evening.

Daler lifts my hand and gently presses his lips to it. "I am very sorry Chakori, but we will need to end the celebration now."

"I understand."

He waves for Emund and some of the other guards over. "Love, go into the house. Your things have been moved into our new room. Today has been very stressful for you. Please go and rest."

"Please, I want to be with you husband?"

He smiles. The word husband delights him.

"We have forever my love, go. I will join you in a little while." A woman I have never met before takes my arm. I look to him.

"This is Giza your new guard, servant, or whatever you may have need for."

Annetta Hobson

I am so afraid, I don't know this woman. I have no reason to trust her. He notices my sudden uneasiness.

"Chakori. She has been with my family for a very long time. I promise you are in good hands. Go . . . I will be with you before you even miss me."

"I miss you already Daler."

He walks over to me and Giza releases my arm. He leans close to my ear and whispers. "I am going to make love to you all night. Please go and get ready for me." He knows I am going to comply with his wishes now. I take Giza's hand and we enter the house.

We walk in the opposite direction of my old room. I have never entered this part of the mansion. We pass several elegantly decorated rooms. I hear sobs and we come to Lady Surina's room. We hurry by I do not want to face her. She is in pieces and I can relate to her. If that were Daler I would be a mess. I walk alongside Giza. I glance at her periodically. She is very serious.

"Here you are Lady Chakori." She stops in front of a room at the very end of the hall. I am a little nervous being at the end of the hall of the family's wing.

"Thank you very much."

"If you need anything I will be at the room across the hall."

I nod and look over to her room. I enter my door and this room is too much for words. It is nothing like the rooms I have slept in since I was brought here. The bed is very large. I tour the room and it is three times the size of the others. I am too tired to enjoy it all so I unzip my extravagant gown. I step out of it, take off my undergarments and slide underneath the lavish bedding. When I am beneath the covers I nestle in. It all feels so incredible against my naked body. Before I realize, I am drifting off.

Chronicles of a Betrothed

When I wake it is morning. I sit up and I am alone. I spent my first night as a First Lady without my husband. I hear water running and then silence.

Daler enters from the bathroom as naked as I am.

"Finally, you are awake."

"Where were you Daler I wanted you here with me. We are husband and wife now. I wanted you here beside me, inside of me."

He laughs out loud. "Calm down, I am afraid I have turned you into quite the seductress. But do not fret I am here now."

He sits on the bed and rubs a towel across his wet hair. He sits on the edge of the bed. I slide up to where he rests. I glide my hands across his back. I lean closer to press my lips against his skin. I suck it in to taste. I slide my tongue along his shoulder. He closes his eyes and reaches for me. He lifts his arm and I lie on his lap. He caresses my hair as it spills down his leg. He stares down at me.

"I think you pretend to love me so much." He whispers.

"I . . . do not pretend." I try to sit back up and he presses my shoulders down back to his thighs.

"I look at you and I wonder why you are here with me. I know you were forced. But you know my darkest secrets, you could have easily…"

"I was forced. But I have grown to love every part of you. There is no other place I long to be. Where ever you go I want to be by your side."

He takes a moment to glare at me.

I reach up, holding his handsome face. I pull it to mine. I greedily take his mouth and he gives in to the hunger. He stands

Annetta Hobson

and scoops me into his arms. I hold on to my husband. I want him to take me. I can give him all of me. The very depth of my soul belongs to him. I motion for him to release my legs, he obliges. I step down and without coming up for air we kiss like hungry wolves. I let my petite hands explore his body. I reach for his firm behind. I massage it. He lets his hands fall to his side. I take that as permission to continue my admiration of his sculptured physique. I feel his want. It presses against my stomach. He is as starved as I am. Our appetite for one another screams from deep inside. My lips halt their assault. I look and I have to answer his body's call. I position myself on the floor. I am on my knees preparing my mouth to pleasure him. I slide my lips around him. He grabs my hair and assists me. He relaxes his neck and his eyes close. I grab his behind and he pushes into my throat. I moan as he enjoys the love I bestow upon him. Before I can coax him to an end, he grabs me by my shoulders and lifts me up. He pushes me back to the bed and I fall onto it.

"Open your legs my love."

They spring open and he gently massages my center.

"This is how it is done."

"I like it better when you touch me." I moan.

I close my eyes to enjoy his touch. He grabs my thigh and presses it back. His unbelievably beautiful face dips deep between my thighs. I moan at the pleasure his mouth gives me. I feel as though I will melt onto perfectly parted lips. He lifts from my valley and I am deliciously hungry for more. He steers himself into me. I moan in delight. I finally have him inside me. I bring my legs up close to my body and he drives deeper. He grips my bottom and rocks in and out. I place my hands on his face. I

Chronicles of a Betrothed

stroke his cheeks and pull his lips to me. We kiss as he thrusts in and out of me. I feel myself on the brink of combustion. The heat builds deep inside of me and I scream out in pleasure. I feel my center clench around him and I pull his love right into me. He groans with exhilaration. We discharge our passion and it mingles together as it seeps from me. He releases my thighs and they flop down. I pull his body to mine.

"Oh Daler I can never get enough of this. Promise me no matter what, I will never have to wait for it." I plead breathlessly.

He smiles my enchanting smile and says. "I promise I am going to give it to you when you like." He exhales. And we lie there caressing one another, knowing that we are within our rights to have each other no matter who knows.

Chapter 16

I walk into the dining area. The family is assembled for dinner and Surina is a wreck. Her eyes are puffy and red. I walk over to her. She looks up to me. My heart aches for her. I used to wonder how she could love a man like Pavan Khattris. But I have fallen for his son and if he was half as charming as Daler I understand. He was the evilest person I have ever known. But Surina loved him with her soul, she loved Monarch Khattris. I place my hands on her shoulders. She grabs one and squeezes it.

"Thank you Chakori. Your presence is greatly appreciated. I see you smiling. You must be enjoying being the wife of a Khattris."

"I am. Daler is wonderful. I will love him all of my days."

Her sad eyes brighten a little. "You discovered this in a single night?"

"No getting to know him was the greatest gift your husband could have given to me. I love the gentle man he has come to be."

"Most likely because of you, my son is a new man since his betrothal to you."

"Thank you."

The sadness in her eyes returns.

Annetta Hobson

Daler enters as I take my seat.

"Mother are you alright? I hear you are not eating."

"I am fine my son. Please do not worry about me. I want you to enjoy your new bride."

"I have the right to worry. I know you adored father."

She sighs as she intertwines her fingers and rests her elbows onto the table. "Daler I absolutely adored him, but feared this day would come. I am just grieving. I will be fine."

"Your strength is very admirable. I am in awe of your grace. I am sure Chakori will make you proud as the new First Lady of the now Islands of Amity. I want to rename them. I want things to be different. They will be called The Jutesh Republic. The people are one now. There is no need to separate them by name anymore.

"Well son, you have been very busy. I know you are a good man Daler. But please do not let power corrupt you. I loved Pavan but he had become a corrupt ruler. Greed and ambition got him killed. Do not follow his actions or you will face the same fate."

"I hear you mother. And thank you. But father and I are two different people."

She rubs the creases in her forehead and stands. "I wish to talk to you Daler. When you finish with your meal, please meet me in the study."

"Yes mother." He responds as he lifts the utensil to eat.

Surina turns to me. "I will see you later First Lady." She nods and then exits.

I am in awe of her myself. I could imagine the pain she feels, yet she is a rock. I pray one day to mirror her elegance and grace.

Chronicles of a Betrothed

I stare at my plate unable to take another bite. The taste of food in my mouth right now sickens me.

"What is it Chakori?" Daler notices my disgust.

"I am fine. I'm just not as hungry as I imagined."

"I really need you to eat love. You are responsible now for more than just you." He says as he spoons food into his mouth.

"I know husband. But if I eat anymore, the food I have eaten will end up on the floor."

He nods. "Understood."

I place my hands into my lap and wait for him to finish his dinner. He watches me as he eats. I fantasize it is me that is the meal. The way the food slides into his mouth with each bite is slowly seducing me. His lips press against the fork and slides out after he has taken it in. His eyes close as he takes the next bite. I imagine the food is tasty. But it cannot be as delectable as I am. I take my napkin and unfold it. I wipe my forehead. The heat that I feel when I look at this man is insane. My thoughts travel to our steamy morning. I want more. I want him to taste me. I want to feel his lips on my body in all places.

"Love, your glare is as intoxicating as your touch. How will I function if you watch me the way you do."

I shake my thoughts away. My expressions are an indicator. "I apologize. My thoughts are far from this room."

"And what room are they in?" He smiles.

I cannot take it. That smile has just rendered me helpless. "Our bedroom."

"And my eating triggered your thought of rooms?"

"No. Your every movement triggers thoughts of what I want you to do to me in rooms."

Annetta Hobson

His eyes grow wide. He coughs into his fist. "Chakori, I fear I will not be able to carry out my duties as long as I am married to you."

"Is that good or bad?"

"Both . . . good because I want to ravish you every second of the day, and bad for the same reason. I will never be able to get anything done."

"I am sure you can balance your time. Satisfy me then tend to your Lands." I playfully state.

He chuckles.

"What have I done to you my innocent bride?"

"You have awakened me. My heart is full and my body wants. I am the happiest I could ever be. Your children grow in my belly, and that is the pinnacle of it all."

"Keep talking like this, and we will not ever leave our bedroom again."

"That would be the highlight of my life."

He pushes his plate away, wipes his mouth with the linen napkin and throws it on the table. He stands and in a blink he is pulling me from my seat. He dives right in. We kiss and I taste sweetness on his lips. He runs his finger through my hair and rests them there. I wrap my arms around him and forget where we are. All I have wanted for months is his affection allday every day.

I hear someone clear their throat. Daler pulls from my lips. I do not budge. My lips stay in position. Passion has enticed me. I do not care who just entered I want his lips back onto mine.

"I apologize for the interruption. I have news for you sir." Emund says as he approaches.

Chronicles of a Betrothed

Daler turns with his hands still locked in my hair. "What is it Emund?"

"Sir, I received some news when the death of your father was announced."

He releases me and I grip the table to calm my hormones. I do not look to Emund. The lust in my eyes may discomfort him.

"About?"

"Well, I received a call from a woman named Shadari Osi."

"I know Shadari she was our governess. I believe father fired her."

"No sir, he did not. According to Ms. Osi, Monarch Khattris employed her elsewhere."

"Alright. And she called because of what?"

"Apparently she has been raising his son."

Daler shakes his head as if dismissing a thought. "His what?"

"She claims Monarch Khattris delivered a baby boy to her one night about 20 years ago. She placed the baby with an elderly lady to care for him. At first she would just visit the baby and help care for him as she did for you and your sisters. Then when he was seven years of age the other caregiver died and she had to take him as her own. She was sworn to secrecy. If anyone was to find out he threatened to have her killed. They have not lived on this island for several years. She got word of your father's death and assumed they would no longer be cared for if she remained silent."

Daler begins to pace. "So who is his . . ." He quickly looks away. He grabs his chin and gently massages it.

I suppose he has an idea of who is this child's mother as do I. He steps away to make a call. Soon he is back at my side.

"So what is she going to do?" Daler asks. His beautiful smile is now replaced with worry and concern.

"She wants to bring him here. She says he works for a living but she will not continue now that Khattris is dead."

"He is 20 years of age. She has no need for my father's assistance."

"According to her, Monarch was responsible for them both until his demise." Emund explains.

Daler continues to pace. "I need to do a bit of digging. I would like to meet with both of them tomorrow morning, set it up for me Emund. Make sure she keeps this between us for now." He nods and exits the dining room.

"Is there a problem?" I ask.

Daler appears grim, his handsome face riddled with angst.

"Nothing you need to worry yourself about my love." He walks over to me and kisses my forehead. I love the way he slides his fingers through my hair and allow his lips to linger on my skin. It forces me to forget any and every thing.

"What would you like to do this evening Chakori?" He asks

"I would like to be with you . . . but I know that you have business to attend to."

"You are correct. So what else would you like to do? I can have Giza take you somewhere."

"No I will just go back to my room and await your return."

"I would rather you not do that. You will find yourself many nights waiting for me Chakori. I do not want you to become bored."

"Too late husband."

Chronicles of a Betrothed

He smiles and wraps his arm around my neck. We walk out of the dining room and start toward the study. His mother wants to speak with him. *Could she know about this illegitimate son of Khattris?* We arrive in front of the study. We step in and Daler walks me over to sit. The back of the study is a full library. There are many dust filled books. That is one of the things that they still own that is out dated. Ninety percent of the libraries in the UC have virtual libraries. Books are mostly extinct in the modernized areas of the world. I study the room as Surina enters.

"Thank you for coming son. I really need to resolve this matter."

Daler has already been hit with enough shocking news for one evening. What could she possibly have to say to him? His brow creases, obviously he feels the same as I do.

"What is it mother, you seem alarmed?"

"I do not know where my beloved husband was killed. I am afraid we may be next. I want to take Jasmine and Jasleen away. I want to go and live a very quiet life where we can be safe."

"What does that mean mother? Jasmine is preparing to move to the United Countries for school. She is still my candidate for Justice of the main courts."

"I know this Daler. But I am afraid for our lives. I am also concerned for you and your new bride." She turns to me. I look to the floor.

"There is no need Mother. You are overreacting. Father had many enemies. That does not mean they will come after us."

"But the treaty . . ."

"I do not believe this was about the treaty. It makes no sense."

"Well, why kill Ciria?"

Annetta Hobson

"Wrong place wrong time."

"Why were they together? Was she his . . ."

"Mother please do not jump to any conclusions. He would never have touched Ciria. Father was consumed by tradition. He considered Ciria as a potential bride, Sorry my dear." He says as he turns to me. "He would have never laid one finger on her."

"I suppose, but there are so many unanswered questions."

"I tell you what mother. Go to the UC. I will have President Hunter put a strict detail on the three of you. That way Jasmine can attend school and you can live without worry."

"I do not know Daler."

"Think about it. Let me know what conclusion you come to."

"I will my son." She walks over to him and embraces him tenderly.

She exits and Daler turns to me. He does not speak. He grabs my hand. I take hold of it. He seems worried. Before I can speak Emund enters.

"Your guest has arrived sir." He pulls me along and I do not protest.

"Were you expecting someone husband?"

Yes but do not worry my darling. Just stand beside me." I nod and we travel through the house down to the foyer. When we arrive Eveleen is standing there. She appears uncomfortable.

"How may I help you young Monarch? Your phone call was very quick and alarming. I have done all you have asked."

He releases my hand and scans the room. He looks down the halls and up the stairs. "I will not keep you long. I have a few questions I need answered."

She sighs. "I am an open book sir." She states sarcastically.

"I heard you speak of a child."

Her eyes widen. She appears unprepared to answer. She clutches her chest and quickly looks to the floor.

"Tell me about the child between you and my father." Daler demands as he searches for witnesses.

"Wait sir." She places her palms in the air.

"My intension is not to hurt you. I just want information."

Her expression turns inquisitive. "I . . . I gave birth to a male child about 20 years ago." I finally understand the reason for her invitation.

"Go on."

"Pavan was present. I had no knowledge of his intension. As I pushed my child from my body . . ." she recalls, pain riddling her beautiful face.

I witness the anxiousness in his eyes.

"When my son was born I heard his cry as he was whisked away. The physician stood aside helpless. I was told by him later the child was killed. He said no one could ever know about him or I would die also. So you see Monarch, every breath I take is closer to my last as long as I am at the service of the Khattris family."

I fear she has over stepped her boundaries. *This family has caused her great pain. And we dare ask her for more service.* My heart is heavy for Dr. Agroia. How has she dealt with the pain of her child's presumed death?

Chapter 17

We stand in the foyer staring at one another. I know she is wondering why Daler is asking a multitude of questions. Her expression holds. She knows that my husband will kill her without thought if necessary.

"Thank you Eveleen. That is all I need from you. I will see you in two weeks when you examine my wife and our babies."

She nods. The pains in her eyes grow.

Daler has dredged very hurtful memories of her beloved son. I watch as she walks out of the door. I feel such grief for her. If anyone were to threaten our children lives I would turn as murderous as my husband. Eveleen has lived a terrible life. Loving Monarch Pavan has caused her great loss. I fear that it is not worth it. When the door closes Daler turns to me.

"I knew it. If she were to ever find out she would have the ultimate leverage over us. She must never discover that her son is alive. He has claim to the leadership of the Islands."

"How? No one can prove he is the son of Monarch Pavan, especially if he never surfaces."

"I like the way you think wife. I must rectify my father's problem immediately."

Annetta Hobson

I stare at him for a moment. He has a look of carnage in his eyes. My heart begins to pound. I clutch my chest to calm myself. *What is it that he is going to do to rectify this matter? I am sure poor Shadari does not know what fate would befall her. Eveleen does not deserve to lose her son twice. After all of the things that she has endured knowing that her son lives would be the highlight of her life. I believe the distaste she has for my husband would lift a little. The fear of her deception would not be a constant threat.* "Daler?" I whisper as we walk hand in hand through the halls of this grand mansion.

"Yes love, what is it?"

I stop walking and he turns to me. He is a bit irritated by my sudden halt.

"Do you think you can just tell Eveleen of her son being alive? She may be grateful and the vendetta against this family would be over."

He sighs. His dark thick eyebrows crease. His beautiful eyes pierce my soul. "My sweet, sweet wife, that is not possible." He says trying to calm himself. I suspect I have crossed a major line.

"If Eveleen were to find out her son lives, she would immediately go to the President and stake his claim as a rightful heir."

"But you are older Daler, he has no claim here, and he is illegitimate."

He releases my hand and places it on my cheek. I lean in and place my hand on top of his.

"Chakori . . . these are not the days of old. If his paternity is proven he may claim a portion and I have committed acts, one getting you pregnant before marriage, which would ensure his reign. So you see my love there is no other solution." He grabs my hand and pulls me along.

I refuse to give up this conversation. I know it will anger him but he wants to kill his own brother, if I am understanding him.

"Daler, this is your brother. What will you do, murder him?"

He huffs but does not look at me.

"Look at me husband you cannot kill this woman's son. It is not right."

He stops, lifts my hand and tosses it back to my side. When he turns to me his eyes are filled with anger. "What gives you the notion that you have any say so in this? I did not ask for your opinion. You should be quiet, make love and have my children. Leave the affairs of these lands to me. That was our arrangement. And do not ever forget it!" He yells.

The harshness of his words ring into my mind, he is correct. I promised to turn my head. I am not a Monarch. I am just his bride. My head drops. I can feel his breath as it hits my hair.

"You think because I did not end Eveleen's life you can order me on what I should do? Make no mistake Chakori I am the one in charge not you. And, because you have leverage between your thighs does not constitute equality!"

His statement stings as it leaves his lips. I cannot believe he said that. I thought it was because he loved me. But now I am just a slave only to make love to him and have offspring. I raise my eyes to his. Tears have begun to stream down my cheeks.

"Well **Sir,** I apologize for assuming I was more than just your child bearing sex slave. I will never make that assumption again." I bend deep to constitute a bow and a curtsy. I clutch my growing belly as I rise. "Now if you excuse me I will go and correct myself for assuming I was a real wife to you." I whisper so that I do not anger him further. But I want to convey the pain he has stricken upon me. When I turn to walk away he grabs my arm. Our eyes meet and I see a bit of sorrow in them.

He begins to speak. "Chakori? Do not…"

I wait. Will *he extend an apology*?

"I will not be joining you this evening love. Giza will be stationed at your room. Good night."

I think that statement hurt worst of all. I know I have crossed a line. I thought we were in love. I believed he would listen to reason but there is none. I walk slowly to my room massaging my hidden swollen stomach. *Has it all been a lie? Or did I just cross a line?* I slowly walk toward my room. My thoughts are everywhere and nowhere. Daler is the very reason I awake in the morning. My love for him is as real as the babies I carry. I feel that Elliot and I would have never shared the passion we produce. My heart aches with each step I take toward the room we share. I do not want to be in there tonight. I spot Giza approaching.

"Good evening Mistress."

"Hello Giza . . . ." Why should I sleep in that room alone? I will not lay in the bed where he made wonderful love to me. I fear that I would long for him the entire night.

"Giza, will you please find and empty room I can rest in. I do not wish to sleep in this area tonight. And please tell no one of it. If anyone asks, I will say it was of my own finding."

"Yes Mistress." She says as she hurries to do my bidding.

I walk over to a plush chair in the hall. I slowly sit as I admire the art work that adorns the walls. All of the rooms in this hall are master suites. My glare leaps from door to door as I think of how

Chronicles of a Betrothed

the man I love spoke to me moments ago. My ducts take control of my eyes, they fill with tears and I allow them to spill onto the fabric of my clothes. I do not wipe, each tear leaves a larger stain. I will always be in the way of his lust for murdering power. *I was a fool to think love could change such a man.* I watch as Giza walks toward me. Her eyes search my face. The tears must alarm her. But she would dare not speak of it.

"Mistress, I have found a room that is accessible. But it is on the east side of the mansion. Monarch would not be happy with me if I allow you to rest in that section."

I press my lips together. Giza and everyone else around here serves him, including me.

"Look I am sleeping wherever I choose this evening. So you can come with me or stay in your room. Either way it makes no difference to me." I stand and wave for her to lead the way. When I arrive to the east side of the mansion I see why she is skeptical. It appears as if the servants sleep in these quarters. They are much better than the rooms in my mansion on Ghatlan. But the one I was locked in the first day I awoke here is much more luxurious. As I walk the hall I scan the walls. There is no fancy art. The walls are bare, painted beautifully, but bare. I hear a door open behind me and I quickly turn. I see that it is the cook leaving his room to use a bathroom at the end of the hall. I suppose they must all share it. When I reach the room I step in. It has a nice large bed. Not as plush as the ones in my former rooms. I sit on it and look to Giza.

"Mistress . . . are you sure you want to do this?"

"Positive. Now you may go if you like."

"No. I will sleep in that chair." She points to a burgundy chair that sits in the corner of the room. I nod and stand to undress. I walk over to a dresser that is positioned next to the chair and rummage through it. I find a gown. It appears as if it is made for an older woman. I slide into it.

"Mistress?" She says as she looks me over. Her face expresses disgust. "Would you like me to go and retrieve your night clothes from your room?"

"No. I am no different than anyone else tonight. My husband has made it clear to me. I work here like the rest of the staff. So I am in perfect company tonight."

She is mortified. I could not shock her anymore tonight with my words.

"Mistress please? I do not want to upset Monarch Khattris."

"I assure you he will know this is my doing not yours. I will take punishment for us both."

Worry riddles her. I am afraid that she will die of it.

"Goodnight Giza." I say as I nestle beneath the covering. I fall asleep as soon as my eyes shut.

I hear the ringing of alarms. My eyes flutter open. I peer at a clock high on the wall and it is virtually dawn. I hear the shuffle of bodies scurrying throughout the halls. They must be on a strict schedule because they hurry off as if going to battle. I look over to Giza who is drifting back off. Her feet dangle down the side of the chair. It appears to be as comfortable as sleeping in a small basket. I turn and snuggle back into a slumber.

When my eyes open again it is almost noon. Giza is awake. She peers out of the small window beside the bed.

"Mistress. You need to eat something. Shall I go and fetch you lunch?" she says as she glances at her watch.

Chronicles of a Betrothed

"No Giza, I am fine. I feel a little sick today." She gives me a grim glare. Sleeping in the service quarters is one thing not eating is another.

"Mistress, I beg of you. Eat." She pleads.

"Alright then. Go and see what you can find." She smiles. Soon she heads out of the door and closes it behind her. I stand, my head begins to swirl. I grab the bed post to keep from falling. I grab my clothing from the day before and look them over. They are quite wrinkled from being folded all evening. I sigh. I do not want to leave this room exposing how I feel. I walk to the door and slowly pull it open. I peek through a small crack. The hall is empty. I step into the hall and make my way to the other side of the mansion. As I walk I search for signs. I know that my husband is aware of my defiance. I get to my room and I nudge at the door. It creeps open. I peek in and the room has no sign of his presence. I rush to bathe. My heart pounds as I rest in the full size bathtub. I think of how I reacted to his harsh words. Soon there are tears falling onto my breasts. The way he spoke to me was inexcusable. I hope he has some type of remorse.

I twist my hair into a bun and lay my head back. It rests on the tub. I slowly close my eyes and let the tears fall. I think of the love I feel for my Tyrant husband and hope that it will always solve our differences. Soon I hear my door to the room open. I know that it is Giza arriving with a meal for me. She had to know that I would come back to my room to clean myself. I would not dare risk anyone walking in on me bathing. My pregnancy would be revealed. I yell out to let her know I am present.

"Giza . . . I will be right out!" I scream to her. I wait a moment, but she does not respond. She must have brought my meal and went to clean herself up. I shake from my rest and wash myself clean. I dry myself off and step into my room. I look around and there is no food and no one there. I wonder who has entered and left. I quickly dress and go in search for my guard. I search for a long while before I find anyone. I step into the main living area and there is a woman and young man present. As I step in and the young man stands.

"Hello," He walks toward me with his hand extended. He is just as beautiful as my Daler. His hair is a bit longer. It is black, wavy and gently rests on his shoulders. He has deep features and thick dark eyebrows. His skin is lighter than my husband's. He must have been in seclusion. He is tall like his father. His eyes are as blue as clear ocean water. I stare for a moment before speaking. *How could anyone deny that this is Pavan's son? His lineage is uncanny. It is like staring at Pavan himself twenty to thirty years ago.*

"Hello. I am Tiran. I am from Mount Sacetra in the United Countries." He smiles a perfect smile. It reminds me of Daler's gorgeous grin. He grabs my hand and shock waves flow through my body.

"I am Chakori, formally of Ghatlan. I am now the first lady of the Jutesh Republic." I shake his hand and we stare at one another for what seems like forever. The woman stands and I do not look at her. She takes a step toward us and our eye contact does not falter.

"And I am Shadari Osi. I am Tiran's Mother." She says with confidence.

I tear my eyes away from his intense glare.

He does not release my hand right away.

"Hello." I say sliding my hand from his.

"I am very impressed with the combinations of the four Islands. Monarch Pavan has desired this unity for several years." She extends me her friendly gesture.

"I am very sad I did not get the chance to meet such a great and history making leader." Tiran states.

"I am also. May I ask where Mount Sacetra is?"

"Yes . . . it is an Island that sits on the line of the UC. It could have almost been one of the Undiscovered Islands. You must visit it one day. I could show you some of the lovely sights. I just wish it had beautiful women like you First Lady Chakori."

I blush. My skin flushes and I am quickly under the spell of another Khattris.

"I appreciate your kind words. I am sure you have no problem with the young women on your island."

"Yes but I have not found any I would give my heart to." His stare deepens.

I turn away because his glare is threatening to haunt me. "Well, it was a pleasure to meet you both. I need to grab a bite to eat please excuse me." I walk to the dining room and they follow.

"We were actually heading to the eating area also. The servant invited us a moment ago."

I nervously laugh. We get to the table, he hurries ahead to grab my chair. He pulls it out and motions for me to sit. I do not look into his eyes again.

"Thank you." I say as I sit.

Annetta Hobson

A servant enters and apologizes for keeping them so long. She asks if they would like something to drink and when they answer she scurries to fetch it.

"Will Monarch Daler be joining us?" He asks.

"I do not know. I have not spoken with him this morning." I say as I spread a linen napkin across my lap."

"Oh . . . I do not mean any disrespect, but I would never leave such a beauty for long. I would have you in my sights 24 hours a day. There would be no reason I would leave your side. I am so sorry but your beauty is captivating." He says smiling brightly.

"Tiran." Shadari states. "That is quite enough. Mistress Khattris is prestigious. You may not speak to her in this manner. People die on this island for such acts." She turns to me. "I am very sorry Mistress, my son has never been in the presence of royalty per say."

"No, no, it is quite alright. I understand. Things are so different in the UC. Please I do not mind." I still do not look to him. I am afraid Daler will catch me looking into his eyes and he will die immediately. The servant brings the meal and we prepare to eat. I search for my husband before I devour my food, but there is no sign of him. I start and the meal is so delicious I moan, each juicy morsel frolics on my lips before sliding down my throat. I close my eyes and I am delighted by the taste. My delight for the meal is interrupted by my memory of the day before. And I stop in my tracks. I try to fight back my urge to cry. I will not let these strangers witness my pain. But for some reason this young man notices.

"Are you alright First Lady?" he places his fork beside his plate. The clink of it hitting the china causes me to look up.

Chronicles of a Betrothed

"I am fine. But please call me Chakori." As I speak Shadari cuts in.

"That would not be appropriate Mistress."

I nod. And slide my chair back.

"I have something to tend to, I hope to see you two again." I can no longer sit in the presence of anyone.

"Oh you will Mistress, your husband has invited us to stay for as long as we wish."

I turn to him. *Why would Daler do such a thing? It makes no sense.* I stand to exit the room he hurries to join me. "Please excuse me. I am retiring for the day."

"Oh please do not leave on our account. I really would like to get to know my new sister-in-law."

I pause. His words shock me. Could he have known the whole time?

"I am so sorry, what do you mean sister-in-law?"

He smiles. "My brother has not disclosed this to you. He has a half-brother. I thought you were aware."

"Oh no, I just did not know you were. I apologize for my rudeness Tiran."

He moves close to me. "It is fine Chakori. I feel privileged to have met you. I am afraid to admit I am a bit jealous of Daler. He has such a stunning wife. I wish I were the one that had the pleasure of being betrothed to such a beauty."

I blush once more. I know this young man is truly a Khattris. He has the power to immobilize any woman with a word.

Chapter 18

Tiran holds on to my hand. I try to pull away but he does not allow me.

"Chakori, may I ask you a question?"

I pause. What could he want to ask me now?

"Yes, please ask anything you like."

"Well . . . I know of my father's deeds. My mother has kept no secrets, with the exception of the identity of my birth mother. That is only because she is unaware. But my question is . . . I have heard of my brother. His reputation does not precede him. Does he hurt you in any way?"

I am appalled by his question. He knows nothing of Daler and me. How dare he assume?

"Why would you think you know anything about my husband, aside from rumors? You have no idea of the man he is."

He steps closer. His expression is serious. He is as handsome as Daler when he is trying to convey his concern.

"I am not trying to insult you Mistress but my mother has told stories of the Khattris family all of my life. I know my brother well. She was their nanny for a very long time. When I needed full time care Monarch Pavan ordered her to do so."

Annetta Hobson

I release my hand from his firm grip. "It was a pleasure meeting you and your mother. I hope you enjoy Jutesh." I nod and turn to leave.

"I am sorry if I have offended you. I hope I have not tarnished my impression. I pray I get the opportunity to make it up to you. I promise I will not disappoint."

I purse my lips. *Who does he think he is? Why does he think he has to make up anything to me?* "You owe me nothing. It is us who owe you."

"I am here to collect. But I do not require much."

His statement confuses me. *What is here to collect then?* I walk away searching for my husband. I wonder aimlessly around the mansion trying to find him. *Where could he be?* I scour the mansion for hours. The day gets away from me. I retire for the evening annoyed and angry, my husband has let me meet his new family alone.

Weeks pass and my belly expands. Daler remains occupied with something I have no knowledge of. I get a tender hello and goodbye, nothing else. I sleep alone each night. My days are filled with bland conversations and false happiness. Lady Surina and her daughters have left the island for the UC. They have been there since a little after the wedding. I miss the ramblings of Jasleen. She had seemed to be my only ally in this whole extreme experience. I do not believe their mother wishes to return. And living in the United Countries is all Jasleen has dreamed of. I will have to go and visit if I wish to see them.

Tiran has a multitude of questions and no answers. He wonders around the mansion as bored as I am. Or at least it appears that way. I am whisked away periodically for visits with Dr.

Chronicles of a Betrothed

Agroia. The visits are the highlight of my life. For I have no one else. Daler is careful to keep Tiran a secret from the rest of Jutesh. He has agreed to remain hidden. I wonder what Daler is up to. Eveleen will know of her son if he continues to play these games. I am lonely, the past week has been the hardest. Our last conversation was the night before Tiran arrived. I spoke coarsely to the man I love. He must be upset with me. He will neither confirm nor deny either. I get nothing from him. I go to bed frustrated as usual.

Tiran worries me a bit. I walk about the mansion tending to my needs. I go outside to the garden sometimes for an adventure or two. Giza cares for me well. I suspect she has gotten a peek of my growing belly but she makes no reference of it. I run into Shadari occasionally but she is a hard character to decipher. They both give me strange attention. I have not witnessed any interaction between Tiran and Daler. I am sure my husband hates that he is still here.

"Hello Mistress. It is a lovely day for a swim. I would love to have company." Tiran says as I pass him in the main hall.

"No thank you. I am afraid I have to pass."

"Come on Chakori. You never do anything. I see you aimlessly wondering the hall day after day with your female goon trailing you. That is no life for a woman like you." He smiles and I hate him for it. He is Daler's opposite. He is always happy, maybe because he did not grow up in the mansion of darkness.

"I do not think so Tiran." I kindly reply.

"Please I just want to see you have some fun." He extends his hand. I turn to scan the hall. It is empty. I grab his hand and shake it gently.

[205]

"I really do not think that is a good idea Daler will . . ."

"We are just siblings having a little fun. Come on I promise I will not give you rest until you accept." He caresses my hand. I quickly pull away.

"I guess it will be alright. Give me twenty minutes to prepare myself." I release his hand and turn to go change.

"We are going to the private beach beyond town. Will that be a problem?" he asks.

"Maybe for you. You are really not allowed to scour the town."

"I was told there is a private road we can take. My mother says it is hidden no one will discover us."

"And, who will drive? Or did you think of that?"

"I will use my mother's vehicle. My brother was kind enough to give her transportation. She is not a hidden secret." He says with a bit of sarcasm.

"Oh I see. I will be at the door to leave in a few minutes."

"I will count the minute's first lady."

"No need for formalities now Tiran."

"You are correct Chakori." He grins as I leave the hall. I take one last glance before turning the corner and he is still watching.

I search my closet and I find a black swimsuit. I purchased it in the UC. I have a beautiful sheer drape to cover myself. I grab a bag and stuff it with a spare set of things to change into. I slide the bag onto my arm and hurry to join him at the door. When I meet him there he has on a pair of swim trunks. His chest is bare. He has a towel dangling around his neck. I watch him as he grabs for the knob. He is physically Daler's match. My husband's body is a bit more defined but they are identical in most ways. Tiran is kind to everyone he meets. I see that he notices my glare. I gather myself and follow him out of the door.

"Mistress! Mistress!" I turn to see Giza running for us. I stop and Tiran grabs my arm and darts out of the door. I look to him surprised by his actions.

"What are you doing?" I ask trying to keep up.

"Surely you can be without your goon for one day." He says chuckling.

"She is here for my protection." I say breathless.

"I assure you I can protect you just the same." He runs and unlocks the doors. He shoves me in and scurries around to jump in. He starts the car and pulls off before Giza reaches the car. I gaze out of the window at her worry filled expression. I know she fears the reprimanding she will receive. I turn in the seat and sit straight.

"Why did you do that to her? She will be punished for losing sight of me." I say.

"She will be fine. I am sure you can persuade your husband to lighten up."

"I do not . . . wait why would you say that?"

"It is just if I were your husband I would be putty in your sweet soft hands."

I blush. His words soothe me. I fear I am taking his inappropriate gesture to substitute my longing for my husband's. We arrive at the beach. I watch the water hit the sand. I am like a child. I have not seen the beach since I left Ghatlan. I am suddenly happy I agreed to come along.

"Beautiful is it not?"

"Glorious. I am so glad I accepted your invitation."

Annetta Hobson

We step from the car leaving our bags behind. Tiran throws his towel into the sand. He runs fast toward the water and dives in.

I laugh at his antics. I see he likes to show his skills. He is an excellent swimmer. I walk slowly toward him to join in. I reach the water and it hits my feet as I remove my shoes. I toss them behind me and search for Tiran. When my eyes find him he is coming up for air flinging the water from his soaked hair. The way he takes his hands and slides them through his hair ignites a fire in me. He wipes the water from his eyes and nose. He waves for me to come in.

"Take off that drape!" He yells. "I know you have a grand swimsuit you want to show off!"

I wave my hand in dismissal. I walk toward the water holding on to my drape. The water rushes me. I start to pick up my pace so it does not throw me back. It feels nice to have a little fun. I sit in the water and let it consume me. I lie back and allow my hair to get soaked. I smooth it back as I come up for air. When I wipe the water from my eyes Tiran is watching me.

"Oh Chakori, why are you so mesmerizing?" He startles me.

He looks to my now hardening breasts. They point in his direction. I fold my arms to cover them. His eyes assault me. He wipes the water away that drizzles down my face. The stare becomes so intense it threatens to entice me. I quickly run and jump into the tide. He follows laughing.

The day passes as we frolic in the cool water. The breeze picks up and I know that it is time to leave. I plunge deep into the water and spring up. When I wipe my eyes I do not see Tiran. I start to make my way back to the shore and he is nowhere in sight.

Chronicles of a Betrothed

I walk up the beach and the sand sticks to my feet. I run to the vehicle and grab the door. I open it and Tiran steps out.

He is absolutely nude.

"I apologize Chakori. I tried to dress while you were still in the water." He says.

I turn my face away as he reaches to grab his things. I feel his hand grasp at my shoulder.

"I know you are alone. I feel your eyes burn through me. Let me give you what you are missing."

I stiffen. His hand caresses my shoulder. It slides down to my arm and I stop it with mine.

"Please do not. You will surely die if you touch another's."

"I am not afraid." He says as he spins me around. He breathes into my face.

I close my eyes to deny the heat burning inside. The truth is I have been deprived. At night my center burns for the attention of my love. But he does not answer. He is away and I fear he does not want to return to me. I hold my eyes shut tight. I feel his breath on my cheek. Then the sensation of his mouth follows. The kiss is sensual. It leaves my cheek tingling. I feel his breath again, but it hits my lips. I turn away and he pulls my chin back.

He brings my lips to his and I do not protest. He kisses me and I let my hands fall to my side. He cradles my face with his hands allowing them to slide into my wet hair. I place my hands on the back of his arms and dive in. The kiss becomes passion filled he pulls me closer and my round belly hits his arousal.

Suddenly, I am dragged back to reality. I carry the children of the man I love. I snatch away quickly.

"I cannot do this! I love my husband." I scream. I run around to enter into the opposite side.

"I am so sorry first lady. Please forgive me. But . . . your beauty hypnotizes me."

I sit in the seat and decide not to change. I fold my arms.

"Take me back to the mansion, now." I command.

He slowly slides on some slacks and steps inside. He starts the engine and drives away.

I stare from the window wallowing in my betrayal. I know Daler will kill him now. And as for me, I am not sure.

"I felt the way you gave into me Chakori. Allow me the chance to show you how you are supposed to be loved. You will not regret it." he whispers.

My mouth drops open. *The nerve of this man is unsettling.*

"No."

"You liked it, I felt it."

"It was a grave mistake that will never happen again." I make it clear I am not interested in pursuing a tryst with my husband's brother.

He stops the vehicle. I can see the mansion from where we sit.

"Let me come to your room tonight. Get rid of your female goon. Allow me to satisfy your burning desire my brother denies."

"Tiran . . ." I plead. "No!"

He sighs.

I hope he gets it now. I will not fold.

He drives me back to the mansion.

Chronicles of a Betrothed

I jump out before he can stop. I grab my bag and storm toward the door.

He hops out to follow allowing me no space.

Giza swings the door open. Her eyes pierce through him as soon as she spots him.

"Monarch Daler would like to have a word with you Mistress. His instructions are for you to call him the moment you arrive."

"Thank you Giza, I will call now." I turn to her before I make my way to my room. "I am very sorry if I caused you any reprimand."

"It is quite alright mistress, I know you tire of having nothing to do. And I also apologize for calling Monarch Khattris."

"No I understand." I nod and she grabs my bag to follow me. I look back and Tiran stands in the door with no shirt on watching me.

I get to my room and grab the phone. I quickly dial my husband.

"Hello! Chakori!"

"Yes Daler." I whisper.

"What were you thinking? I have been going out of my mind. Where were you and why did you ditch Giza? She is there to protect you."

"I know. I just went for a swim . . ."

He interrupts. "Do not let it happen again. Do you understand me love?"

"Yes, I do."

"Good. I will see you later." He says.

"I love and miss you husband. When . . ."

He ends the call before I can get my words out.

Annetta Hobson

I toss the phone across the room and sigh. I try not to cry but it is in my nature. I am weak so all I have is my tears. Each night for days after I cry myself to sleep. I steer clear of Tiran he is a constant reminder. I need Daler and I need him now.

Chapter 19

I wake up early. My eyes adjust to the morning light. I look at my clock and I realize it is my birthday. *I am finally 20 years old. I thought I would feel different at this time of liberation. Today, I will find out what the sexes of my babies are. I hope that my husband will join me. I need him. I long for him to come into my room in the night and take me.* But after all of the time that has past I fear he has another. My eyes react to my heart and begin to pour. I bathe, dress and call to Giza to escort me to my appointment. I know Giza is agitated with me for what I have done but she shows no sign of it. She comes to my room and lets me know it is time to leave.

We make our way through town. The sights change with the seasons. It never gets cold but the sky looks very different. When we reach Dr. Agroia's office we enter. She is patiently waiting never smiling. I know she hates me as much as she hates Daler. The fact I saved her life does not factor into her hate filled mind.

"Good morning Mistress Chakori."

"Good morning Eveleen."

"Undress and sit on the exam table." She says.

I remove all of my clothes except for my bra. I slide into one of the gowns that is folded on the table. When I am done I sit where she asked. I lie back. She presses on my stomach and listens as she usually does.

"Will your husband join us today? Or will we be alone again?"

"Alone again." I return trying not to burst into my usual sea of tears. When she places the device on my belly to monitor the heartbeats I hear nothing. I lift my head to peer at her. She looks at me and speaks.

"Do not be alarmed. They may have moved out of my range, let's just start the ultrasound."

She pours the clear liquid onto my belly and places the handle onto my abdomen. I see my babies clear. The one closest has its eyes shut. I am amazed how clearly I see them. It is as if I can reach in and touch them. I smile, the thought of holding them excites me. I look to Eveleen and she does not share my enthusiasm. I understand having her child ripped from her is a constant pain she relives daily.

"Can you see what they are?"

"Yes. You have a boy and a girl." I manage a smile and allow my tears to escape. *I have a son to carry on my husband's legacy and a daughter to carry my own.*

"Daler will be so happy. I cannot wait to tell him." I try to exude excitement. The feeling does not attach to Eveleen. Her expression is as stone. She cleans my stomach and I sit up. "Doctor. I know that this is hard for you but I am so grateful to you . . ." she lifts a hand to halt my speaking.

"Chakori I have grave news for you." I clutch my chest. *What could she have to tell me? I do not want to know anything that will upset me.*

Chronicles of a Betrothed

"Please Eveleen I cannot handle any news that will upset me." I search her face for a sign, I am hoping her mood lightens.

"I am sorry you are here alone to get this kind of news." My heart starts to race. It pounds so hard I feels as if it will burst through my flesh. I clutch the gown. I stand so I can brace myself for the news she speaks of.

"Dr. Agroia please . . . what is the problem?"

She approaches me with caution. I stare as she moves toward me. I pace myself for her words.

"Chakori," she says folding her arms into one another. "Your babies are not alive. They died in your stomach about two weeks ago. I am very sorry for your loss but we need you to go straight to the hospital. I need to have them removed."

I scream. "No!!!!!!" My heart is breaking I cannot contain my grief. I have lost too much in this short life of mine. She speaks as if she is talking about animals or a pest of some sort.

"Are you sure." I say with tears continuously falling from my eyes.

"Yes there are no heartbeats, and no life in these children."

"Why??" I sob. "What could have happened?" I can barely speak. My heart chokes me.

"I do not know. I have to get them out first so I can find out." I wince at the sound of her voice.

"I slowly walk to the restroom. I shut the door and lean against it. The tears come faster. I shudder from my wailing. I look to my stomach. The perfect round shape deceives me. *My beautiful babies are no more. The dream of our perfect family has now shattered into many pieces. The life inside of my body is no more.* I caress my lifeless belly. I slide to the floor cradling my

Annetta Hobson

children. *They will never inhale the damp island air of Jutesh.* I let my tears fall. The coolness from the marble floor presses against my bottom. I lean my head back to rest it on the door and my soul leaves me for a moment. I close my eyes and the life imagined leaves me one memory at a time. Suddenly I hear a banging on the door.

"Chakori I need you to get dressed now. We have to go to the hospital." She yells through the door.

"I will be right out." I manage to get out with my voice shaking, barely above a whisper.

I dress very slowly and soon I am on my way to the hospital. I peer out of the window of the vehicle. Giza drives and Eveleen follows. I hold my belly knowing soon it will be empty and I will not be a mother. The tears will not stop. I do not think I want them to. I wonder if Daler will come to be by my side.

"Giza, have you got in touch with Monarch Khattris yet?"

"No Mistress, I have not. I have also tried Emund and there is no answer."

I fold my arm and rest it on the base of the window. I place my chin on it and the tears stream down.

We arrive at the hospital and even though I did not expect to be visiting so early. It is well built and Eveleen's picture is the pinnacle of the entry hall. I am wheeled in by a group of nurses I am prepped for surgery. I cry and I cry. There is no comfort for me. Soon my babies will be out of their holding place. I am wheeled to the operating room. My eyes close and I drift away.

When I wake I am in a private room. I look around and I am still alone. I rub my invisibly stitched belly and sob. It has return to its previous flat state. I am overcome with sadness and I have no one to share my misery. I cannot help but think I brought all of this upon myself. *The betrayal I committed has come back to haunt me and somehow I know I do not get to have a happy ending.*

"Knock, knock."

I turn to see who has entered my room.

"I am so sorry to bother you but I heard of your hospitalization by Dr. Agroia." Tiran says entering my room with an alluring smile.

"You talked to Eveleen?" I say as I try to sit up right. The soreness strikes me and I allow my head to fall back to my pillow.

"Yes, I am afraid I did not know you were pregnant."

"And who told you that?" He smiles. My question somehow amuses him.

"I am just a little aware of what goes on in the Khattris Mansion now."

"And what else do you know?"

He walks over to the chair beside my bed and sit.

"I know enough Chakori. How did your husband deal with the news of our little day at the beach?"

"I did not tell him. I would not dare inform him of my unfaithfulness over the phone."

"Oh I see. And, is there a reason he has not rushed here to be by your side."

"I am sure he will be here shortly." I say clutching my gown close to my chest.

He shakes his head. "I do not think so Chakori. Your husband is in the UC."

I turn my head to look away from him. It seems as if he is enjoying my pain.

"You should be a little more kind to me Chakori." He says sarcastically.

"And why is that, Tiran?"

"I, and my Mother, will be running Jutesh shortly and if you are nice to me I will keep you as one of my mistresses."

I gasp at his words. I sit up and ignore the pain that surges through my body. The sweet polite man has disappeared and been replaced with the man who sits here beside me, resembling his tyrant father.

"What do you mean Tiran? Shadari cannot run this island, besides Daler is the ruler here."

He laughs, it is heart wrenching. "I know everything Chakori. Eveleen, Pavan, Ciria, everything"

I am shocked he is not the unknowing kind man I frolicked on the beach with not long ago. "I do not know what you are referring to."

"I am sure you know." He says as he stands. He grabs my hand and squeezes tight.

"You will find out everything shortly. You have been in here for three days and my dear brother and his guard are gone. So I am going to make my move, with help of course. You will be here for a while thanks to Dr. Agroia, my mother. It was just evil to kill your babies but she had to strike while he was away. You have softened him up you know. We never could have done all of this without you. I was sure he would kill me. But Eveleen assured me you would not allow it. I think he is upset with you for making him so soft."

I do not speak I am in total shock. Eveleen did exactly what Daler said she would. "How long have you been planning this?" I ask, my voice shaking.

"Well . . . let's see, you had him spare my mother. She contacted me as soon as that happened. We have been in touch for years. My father would come and visit me and then my mother. She found out about me when she had him trailed. We did not know how we would strike but when your husband murdered him we accepted that as a way in. He deserved to die for denying me my birthright."

Do any men in the Khattris family have empathy? This family is full of male mongrels.

"Where is Giza?"

"Dead."

I cover my mouth to stifle my scream. "Why did you kill Giza?"

"Oh no, I would never kill anyone. It was Shadari. She has always taken care of the things I would not. She has served me well for as long as I could make money for her. Now, I will give her everything Monarch Pavan promised."

I sob, my worst nightmare has come true. Everything I have imagined in a nightmare, has materialized.

"Do not cry sweet Chakori. I will not let you die. I warned Eveleen if she harmed you I would not follow through with any of this. I really tried to get you to give in to me willingly. I thought you were going to falter at the beach but I felt your pregnant stomach hit me and I knew you were out. It is too bad you have so much integrity. But I know you are lonely or you would not have allowed me to taste those wonderful lips of yours."

"I have to go to the restroom please." I sob and stand slowly. The pain is stifling but I press through.

"Of course. I will wait here. My mother will be in here soon so hurry. She told me not to let you out of my sight."

I nod and slowly walk to the bathroom. I close the door. *What will I do? I fear Daler is dead. How could he not come to me? He has to be dead and now. I will be Tiran's whore.* I weep constantly. *I will never be anything as long as I am connected to this family. I spot my jacket hanging on the door. I run to it and quickly ramble through the pockets. Could I be so lucky? Could they have left my phone in the pocket?* I find it stuffed away beneath a sea of tissues. Daler ordered me to have one with me whenever I leave the mansion since the beach incident. I believe she did not take it out because she was going to kill me in surgery. Or maybe she just did not look. Why she kept me alive could only be explained by her needing to please Tiran, her son. I dial on the phone quickly. It rings and I hear his sweet, sweet voice.

"Chakori?"

"Oh, Yes Daler. I am so happy you answered. Please listen to me, your brother and Eveleen are trying to replace you. I am so sorry you were right."

"Calm down love you are speaking fast. Where are you?" he asks.

I begin to sniffle I am so glad to hear his voice. The sounds begins to echo throughout the restroom. Soon Tiran knocks.

"Are you alright in there? Do I have to come in and get you?"

"No, no Tiran I'll be out," I yell and return to my call. "Daler they killed our babies and Giza. I believe she wants me dead. But

Tiran has convinced her to keep me for his personal pleasure. Where are you?"

"No!" He states and for a moment he is silent.

"Daler please say something I do not have much time."

"I am so sorry Chakori. I thought Giza could protect you. I did not think Eveleen would be so stupid. I am almost there. I had business in the UC. I was very careful about letting anyone know when I would return."

"How long before you return? They say days Daler, how long?" I yell, in a whisper.

"Darling I am so sorry, I was just giving you what you wanted. Now they are trying to take everything from me. Edmund." He calls into his back ground. "Call the guard and have him kill her brother's wife and child. But tell him to do it quietly. I will show no mercy . . . Chakori?"

"Yes . . ." I stutter

"I am almost there. Please do not get yourself killed you are all I have left."

I sniff. My tears start again. "I love you Daler please come back I need you."

"I will be there in less than an hour."

"Oh god thank you. I will not rest easy until I am in your arms."

He ends the call.

I feel that I will be safe soon. I hide the phone in my jacket and open the door. Tiran is waiting for me. I slide pass him and he watches me.

Chapter 20

"Did you clean yourself up in there beautiful?" Tiran asks. His eyes follow me, I feel naked in front of him.

"I did." I answer.

"I really want you. I want you so bad. When I touched your wet skin that day I knew I would have to enter you. I hoped you would give in and call me to your room. I lie in bed at night hoping for a knock from you. It is all I can think about. And, now there are no babies in my way. When Daler returns in three days we will be waiting to end his world."

"You have already ended our world. I am just an accessory. And, how do you know when he is returning?"

"Oh, you are no accessary my dear. Daler loves you and I understand why. And, to answer your question, we have reliable resources. How do you think we made it thus far?"

"I do not know." I make it to my bed.

Tiran trails me.

"We could have never got away with any of this if you had not come to Jutesh. I owe all of this to you. The day you arrived was the day my mother says she felt hope. Hope to have the opportunity to finally take everything from this family. And return to the Khattris' what they have inflicted on everyone else. They will pay for all of the misery they have caused."

As I sit, I moan from the pain that flows through me. I look to Tiran. He is watching me like a meal. I try to ignore the desire in his eyes but it is so disturbing. I recognize it because Daler wears the same face as this man.

"But look at what she has caused. First lady Surina, did nothing to her. Yet she seduced and had a child with her husband. I heard her threaten to kill her."

"No matter. She has her reasons and I have mine."

He hovers over me, licking his lips like his is preparing to eat. "My mother tells me you are well enough to perform. I am untouched you know. I have saved myself for a woman such as you."

"I do not believe you. As a matter of fact, I hear you are quite the charmer."

He smiles. "Mother . . . I mean Shadari would not allow it. She wanted me to have more than my brother. She says he used women for pleasure. I want more." He caresses my hair and then smells it. I wrap my arms around myself and wait for my husband to rescue me.

"You smell absolutely divine Chakori. Please make this pleasurable for me. I want you to live."

I close my eyes as his hands move down my back. Soon, I feel his hands on my skin moving down to places only Daler should touch. I open my eyes to look at him. He has shut his to enjoy the feeling of my body.

"I've longed to feel you since I first met you. Why should Daler have you? I will love you even if you cannot be my wife."

Chronicles of a Betrothed

I let the faucet of tears flow. The tables have turned. I am being punished for loving a murderer. Tiran takes my hands and pulls them from me. He kneels down and places my hands in his hair.

"Massage my scalp. Run your fingers through my hair." He demands.

He releases my hands. I touch his hair. I slide my hands through his silky mane. The curls bounce with each stroke. I feel for him. He is a pawn, the center of a plot to take revenge. He lays his head on my lap. I continue to caress him. I feel his hands creeping up my thighs. I cringe from the connection of our skin. He moans as his hands assault me. They reach my bottom. I stiffen. He starts to kiss my thigh. He takes one hand and slides my gown up. He kisses gently and then becomes more aggressive. I fist his hair and try to lift his head from my leg but he does not budge. He moans as his lips slide up my thigh toward their destination.

"Lie back onto the bed." He commands lifting his eyes to mine.

I wince once more from the pain as I lie back. He stands and reaches up my gown at my underwear. He gently pulls them down and off. I try to be strong but I cannot. I do not want this man to enter me. *My body is Daler's.*

"I want this to be everything I imagined, I long to feel your insides around me. I stroke my manhood in the night and release my seed into the emptiness. I want to put all of me inside of you. You will bare my children now. My mother guarantees it."

Annetta Hobson

Oh no! I cannot believe this is happening. My womb is not vacated a few days and he wants to replace my children. The flood gates open and the tears are overwhelming.

"Why are you crying? I am putting a child back into your belly. You should rejoice."

Anger builds. I see red and I want this man dead. I cannot believe his logic. He thinks he is giving me what I want. He undresses and mounts me. I lock my legs so he may not enter.

"Please do not make me hurt you. Open your legs. I want my first time to be intimate. I do not wish to fight you. Open them now or I will hurt you." He says disturbingly calm.

"Please Tiran. There are plenty of women who will gladly give you what you want and need."

"I want no one but you."

He leans in and kisses my lips. The taste of his mouth makes me ill. I turn away. He lifts his hand and

"Smack!" he slaps my face hard. I grab my cheek. I have not been struck since I was disrespectful to my father, almost a year ago by Pavan. I wail. The sound escapes me and I scream for dear life.

"Quiet! Quiet! You will alert the whole hospital."

I scream louder. He covers my mouth and I scream through his hands.

"Shut up Chakori!" he places his hands around my neck and begins to choke me. My screams are muffled. I gag at the crushing of my vocal chords.

"I will have you!" He takes one hand from my throat and grabs himself. He takes his knee and plunges it into my thighs they spring open. He quickly tries to enter me. I manage to get

Chronicles of a Betrothed

my knee up into a position to kick him. I aim at his erection. I strike as hard as I can. He releases me and tumbles over the side of the bed onto the floor screaming. I hurry to my feet and look for something to protect myself with. I look at Tiran and he is naked and rolling around on the floor.

"I am going to kill you!" He says clutching himself.

I run to the door and it is locked from the outside. I bang on the door. I see a few people walking around but no one responds. I spot a sign on the wall that reads Psychiatric Unit. No one will let me out. They think that I am insane. I run back to my bed. The room is virtually empty. Tiran is beginning to stand. I circle the bed and grab the chair.

"What are you going to do with that?" He says preparing to stand. I raise the wooden chair high into the air, and slam it down onto his head. He collapses.

"You are going to pay for that!" He growls.

I strike again. I do not stop. I strike again and again. He moans I strike harder. I put force behind each blow until his body is lifeless. Blood pools around his head. The chair shatters into pieces. I back into the wall and look down at my blood stained gown. I killed a man, my husband's brother. I slide down the wall and watch as his blood covers the marble floor. Suddenly I hear a phone ringing. I jump to my feet and search for the sound. It is coming from his pants. I retrieve it and answer without speaking.

"Hello my son. I need you to kill her. Daler is here and I am leaving the island. Are you there? Are you still in her room? You cannot speak? Okay. Meet me at my private airport we leave in 45 minutes. Please hurry you are the only family I have left. Shadari is with me. We will have our revenge in the future . . .

they killed my baby niece, she and her mother are dead." Eveleen sobs.

"Please make a sound so I know you are alright Tiran, I cannot bear the thought of losing you a second time." She pleads.

I end the call. My husband is here. I quickly dial him.

"Hello?"

"Daler my love please come and get me. I am in the Psychiatric Unit. I have killed Tiran please come to me!" I shout.

"Oh God love how? Why? Do not worry I am already entering the hospital. Emund will take care of the mess." The phone goes silent.

I pace the room, waiting for my husband to rescue me. Soon I hear shouting in the hall.

"How in the hell did my wife end up in this unit! Where is she?" I run to the door. I peek out of the window and I see his handsome angry face. He charges toward my room, everyone scatters.

"Open this damn door now!!" A woman grabs some keys and hurries to the door and unlocks it. I have never heard Daler lose control. I have only witnessed him calmly eliminate. This is not like my mild mannered husband. He pushes the door open and when his eyes land on me he gasps. Rage fills his face. I run and jump into his arms.

"Daler please forgive me I will never question you again, I promise my love never."

He cradles me. Caressing, my lose stringy hair. All of the love I have missed is deposited back into me in one sweep of emotion. I am back in the arms of the man I love.

Chronicles of a Betrothed

"I should not have abandoned you Chakori. My pride caused this. I was angry because you have control over me. Your every wish is my command. I am yours to govern."

His words astound me. I am speechless. "You have avoided me because . . ."

"I did not want you to know the power you have over me. Chakori, you possess me. I am yours to dominate."

"I do not want to dominate you. I just want to be your wife. I want to bare you children." With those words my heart sinks. I can tell from his expression he feels the same wrenching pain for lost our babies.

"I will kill her this time I swear. Emund have this mess cleaned up I will meet you at the car." He carries me down the hall and to the vehicle. He slides me inside and I slide over. The pain in my belly subsides at his touch.

"You look a mess love. I will have you cleaned up immediately."

"Daler!" I yell.

"What is it Chakori?"

"Eveleen and Shadari have been involved for a while. They have plotted this for a long time. She is on her way to her private airport as we speak."

He clinches his jaw. I can see the vein pulsating at his temple. Soon Edmund exits the hospital and enters the vehicle.

"Emund, take my wife to the mansion we have to get Eveleen before she boards her plane."

"No! I am going with you Daler. She killed my babies I want to see her!"

He searches my face for any sign of humility. But there is none. She has taken her revenge out on me and I was the one who helped her. I should not have been the center of her plan. She knew I was Daler's world and she tried to destroy him by using me and my children.

"Alright but . . ."

"No mercy this time." I say with no emotion. He grabs my hand.

"Chakori . . . please do not allow your pure nature to be overrun by malice."

"I can identify with her rage. Your father took her child. She has the right to want justice. But now, I will take mine."

He grabs my hand and squeezes it. He takes his other hand and slowly strokes my empty stomach. He closes his eyes and a single tear escapes. I quickly wipe it away.

"I shouldn't have left you to deal with this alone. I will spend the rest of my life making you whole again."

"You owe me nothing Daler. I asked you to spare someone who was a direct threat to our family. I will leave you to make the decisions from this day forward." I turn to look out of the window and I notice that we are approaching the private airport.

"Pull around here Emund and park." Daler points.

"Stay in the car you hear me love. You have had enough of this for a lifetime."

I nod. But I have no intension to stay put. Emund pulls besides a strip of trees. He and Daler step from the vehicle and quietly creep toward the landing strip. After they disappear, I search the front cab. I know Emund keeps a gun beneath the armrest. I find it and attempt to open it to make sure it is loaded. When I am

Chronicles of a Betrothed

confident I can use it I slide my gown off and place it on backwards. I tie it tight as possible so that I will not reveal my half nude body to anyone else. I hurry from the vehicle careful not to be seen. I spot Eveleen running to the plane, Shadari trailing behind her. I search for Daler and Emund and they are not in sight. I race for the plane before the door shuts. I stay low and creep up the stairs and into the cabin. I look around I hear voices but I do not see anyone yet. I glance out of the window and I see Daler in the distance.

"Where is he Eveleen? I need Tiran to make it."

"Hold on Shadari, he will be here, I guess he wanted to experience the Monarch's wife first."

"Are you serious? Daler will hunt us down and murder us all. I am calling him again."

"Daler cannot reach us if we are in the United Countries. He would not dare defy President Hunter."

"If we make it." Shadari says dialing Tiran.

"No answer Eveleen. Are you sure he is alright?"

"Daler could not have possibly made it there before he could leave. I doubt Chakori has the strength to fend him off. I made sure she would be immobile for days."

"Did you have to kill the babies? They were the only innocent ones in this, and she did save your life."

"I thought about it. But she was the only option I had to hurt them the way they have hurt me. I did not get to launch my entire plan. But the defilement of his wife, and the death of the twins, will suffice."

"I suppose he will suffer enough. But I assure you he will never stop looking for us."

"I hope Tiran is safe, I was just sent a message Daler retrieved his bride and they killed an orderly."

"Oh God! Tiran!" Shadari yells. She dials his number once more.

"He is not going to answer." I say.

They both turn to face me. They scan my body and notice I am covered in blood. Eveleen slaps her hand over her mouth.

"Chakori?" Shadari says as her eyes search behind me for my husband.

"Oh what happened to respect? What happened to Mistress Chakori? REVEREVCE ME!" I scream wild-eyed.

They both jump at the fury in my voice.

"Oh Mistress . . ." Eveleen says. "You should not be out of bed. You just suffered a terrible lost. I should know."

"Please do not antagonize me Dr. Agroia. Your feeble son revealed your whole plan before he attempted to take me."

She drops her head. "Where is Tiran now Chakori? You are aware he is the only family I have left. Your husband killed my young niece and her mother."

I do not falter. I keep my eyes locked on them both. "And you killed my babies. After all I tried to do for you. I convinced Daler to keep Tiran alive for you. And you pulled my babies from my body to kill them."

"WHERE IS TIRAN CHAKORI!!!!!!?" She screams, tears and saliva flying from her.

"Lower your voice. You have no right to grieve."

"Is he dead Mistress?" Shadari interjects. I look to her my eyes wild like an animal. I have lost all sense of self-control.

Chronicles of a Betrothed

"Yes. As dead as you will be." Their eyes widen. Eveleen raises her hands.

"Wait, wait just let us leave. We will never . . ." Before she can finish I shoot Shadari three times directly in the forehead. She falls to the ground. Eveleen screams.

"Oh my god Chakori! What are you doing? This is not you."

I turn the gun on her she backs away with her hands raised. The pilot steps from the cockpit and I shoot him immediately before he can speak. He stumbles back and falls to the floor.

"Chakori wait please, I understand your pain. I had no intension of hurting you I swear."

"Shut up now!" I point the gun at her. I see her eyes leave me. I turn to Daler. He grabs my hand and lowers the gun. Sadness washes his face. He slides it from my fingers and hands it to Emund who is directly behind him.

"I told you to stay in the car my love." He whispers. He opens his arms and I fall into them. He holds me tight and I weep again. I let all of experiences from the day I step foot onto this island spill onto his fine suit jacket. He gently rubs my hair. I hear an echo of sobs behind me and I turn to see Eveleen. I do not feel the sorrow I felt for her in her office that day. I know this family created her but she is beyond pity. She will always try to hurt us. I do not deny that now. Daler pulls me away from his body and hands me over to Emund. He grabs my arm and holds it firmly.

"Please Daler . . . let me explain."

"Explain what? You have hurt the closest thing to my heart. You have corrupted her. She is now like us. I never wanted that. But I understand you needed to do this. So I am positive you understand what I have to do. Am I correct?"

Annetta Hobson

"Yes ssssir . . . I do." She says sobbing. "But, is there anything I can say to change your mind. I can go to the UC and you will never hear from me."

"No. My Mother and sisters are there, I will not let you hurt anymore of my family." He reaches for his ankle. The harness strapped to his ankle is visible. He yanks the knife out. She is shivering.

"I . . . I . . . I"

"Shhh . . . do not beg. It is over." He grabs her shoulder. "Your son tried to take my wife. Were you aware of it? Please do not lie. This will decide if you die fast or slowly."

"Yes, I encouraged it. He was untouched. I wanted him to be a man. He chose your wife. He was in love with her."

Rage builds as she speaks. Daler clinches his jaw and I know it is almost over.

He looks to me.

I turn away into Emund chest. I bury my face deep into his jacket. I hear a thud and Eveleen gasps. I look up and Daler is holding her as she falls to the floor. He twists the knife with force. The light in her eyes fades. He yanks the knife from her chest. He wipes it cleans on her tailored suit. I look at her exquisite shoes as blood soaks the carpet beneath them. I feel an unbelievable relief wash over me. Daler places his knife back into the holster and unstraps it. He lifts it toward me and tosses it across the cabin. He then pulls me to him.

"I will never kill again Chakori. If there is no direct threat to our lives, I will never take another life I swear this to you."

I smile. I know he means every word and I am delighted.

"I want to go home Daler." He wraps his arm around me and we leave the plane behind. Emund stays behind and when we reach the car, we hear the plane explode. Emund emerges from the smoke and we leave behind the most horrific experience I think I will ever have.

Chapter 21

We reach the mansion and it is virtually empty. I think of Giza and her life being taken for associating with the Khattris family. I go up to my room and I shower. I wrap myself in a towel and step into my room. I think about my two little angels and how life would have been with them in it. Eveleen stole that from me. And because of that, she is dead. I revel in my revenge. No one will ever take from me again. I turn to walk to my bed and Daler is naked and waiting. He peels the covers back and pats the spot beside him. I drop my towel and join him. I snuggle next to his perfect physique. The warmth of his skin soothes my aching body. I dispose of everything that defiles my mind and enjoy the touch of my beloved husband.

"Are you alright love?"

"Now that you are in our bed I am better than alright."

He chuckles. "All you wanted was for me to come to bed? After the way I spoke to you?"

"Yes, I want you beside me and inside of me all the time. I know by you being the Monarch of the Jutesh Republic we cannot be together all the time. But I want to travel with you and go where you go. Do not hide my eyes from anything else. We are in this together."

"I want to take you and make love until you collapse from pleasure. I want to put you to sleep tonight Chakori. I miss your touch, the feel of your skin escapes me. I have been miserable without you. Let our bodies reacquaint the other then we can talk."

"There is nothing else I would rather be doing." I nod.

His words delight me. I lean up to his perfect face and softly kiss his lips. His hands caress my back. The feeling sends me into space. I am back in the clouds where he first had me. I climb him and the sight of his face is climatic. The way his hair is sprawled across my pillow delights me. He reaches up and slides his thumb along my jawline.

"No woman has ever made me feel the way you do. I am yours forever. No other will ever take your place."

I fight the tears that threaten to surface. I want this to be a tear free occasion. I want to bask in the glory of our love. I lean in to kiss him again. He grabs a fist full of my locks and greedily indulge. We assault one another. The last time our bodies touched was far too long ago. I feel him rise beneath me. I have longed for him to plunge deep inside of me. He reaches down between us I stop his hand.

"Let me." I command. He smiles and lifts his hands in surrender. I take him and place him inside of me. We both let a sigh of relief. I start to rock and swivel my hips. Small stints of pain attack my womb but it will not stop me tonight. I want him, it is all I have wanted besides his love. I rock and thrusts my hips I want to catch a rhythm but I ignore it, the feeling has me on a high. I move my body to the joyous sound of his moans. They are music to my ears. I rock softly but quickly. As I move he sits up to meet my lips. He embraces me and we rock together. I try to hold my ecstasy in but the absence of him inside me gives way and I lose control. My end bursts from me and surrounds him causing him to loudly follow. My crescendo of moans drowns out his, and he drops back to the pillow and my body falls onto his chest. We lie there breathing ragged, enjoying the feeling of pleasures only we share with one another. He folds his arms around me and I plant soft kisses on his beautiful soft skin. He leans up and I lie on my back. He traces the line of my scar with a single finger. I feel the pain resonate through him. He misses my growing belly as much as I do.

Soon I begin to drift off into a quiet wonderful slumber and he nudges me.

"Chakori?"

"Yes husband."

I feel him smile at my words. "I have something to tell you."

"I am listening."

"No love, sit up. I feel you falling asleep. I cannot hold my secret any longer."

I sigh and sit up my hair falls into my face and covers my eyes. He runs his fingers through it and gently pushes it away so I can see.

"Please hide your breast love I really need to concentrate on our conversation."

I grab the coverings and shield my breasts from his immediate sight. I look into his eyes to let him know I am listening.

Annetta Hobson

"I have made some decisions and acted on them. That is why I was away. No one knew why, not even Emund. I did not want any backlash from my constituents."

I run my hand through my hair and straighten my back. "What have you done Daler?"

"I have done all that I have to keep you."

"And, what is that?"

"I signed the islands over to the UC. It is something my father discussed with President Hunter. We are now United Countries citizens. I will be only a local politician. No major decisions will be made by me. We do not have to worry Chakori. We can keep all of our money and we have been granted diplomatic immunity. I will never be arrested for the murders and crimes my family has committed. I want to have a family and be a real father to my future children. No one will ever be allowed to hurt you again. You can have me all day every day. How is that?" He touches the tip of my nose.

I clutch my mouth. My screams radiate through the room I jump up and down on the bed. My breast bounce and Daler's smile is replaced with parted lips. I bend to clutch my belly. He licks his lips and his eyes let me know that he wants me once more. He pulls me down and climbs on top of me. He makes love to me until my legs are tired and shaking. I lay in his arms after our sessions beaming from the news of our new unexpected life. His breathing slows and I know that he has fallen asleep.

I pray that his seed has taken its journey to my womb and planted there. My life can be what I have dreamed it could. I take one more look at my ridiculously gorgeous husband and the serenity he exudes is something he can indulge in now. No more

Chronicles of a Betrothed

murdering plots and secret assassinations. I take my petite hand and slide my fingers across his lips. The joy I feel cannot be contained. I am finally on my way to an abundance of happiness and love. I snuggle into his arms and before I fall into my dreams I note that this is the beginning of a new chapter of life. I thank my father for what he has given me. No matter the road I traveled to arrive, I am no longer just Chakori Desai his betrothed. I am Chakori Khattris, his wife and this is where I belong.

About the Author

Annetta is a Romance Novelist from Detroit Michigan. As a woman with a modern urban personality, Annetta has a firm grasp on the wiles of romance, dating and love. She shares these through her intimate characters who deliver naughty and nice tendencies with an extra dose of sugar and spice.

Annetta Hobson

Her newest title release, "Chronicles of a Betrothed" you have just finished reading, additional titles include:
- Chronicles of a Betrothed
- Light in the Shadow, Part I
- Light in the Shadow, Part II
- Pretty Dreamer
- Reverse Seduction
- The Flame
- Weather Vain

Currently, Ms. Hobson is attending college pursuing a criminal justice major.

She has been married for eleven years and shares seven children with her husband. She loves to read and write.

Visit the Author

Social Media

FaceBook:
https://www.facebook.com/AuthorAnnettaHobson

Twitter:
http://www.twitter.com/AuthorAHobson

Blog and Websites

Wordpress Blog:
http://annettahobson.wordpress.com

Website:
authorannettahobson.org

Publisher

DonnaInk Publications:
http://www.donnaink.org

dpInk
DonnaInk Publications, L.L.C.
www.donnaink.org

Publisher
www.donnaink.org

For more information: bulk orders and/or marketing and promotions contact the Special Markets Division of Donnalnk Publications, L.L.C. at special_markets@donnaink.org and/or http://www.donnaink.org.

ZENCON ART OF ZEN CONSULTANCY

PR & Marketing
www.zenconartofzen.com